HIRING

70 TIMELESS LESSONS AND
TRANSFORMATIONAL STORIES ON RECRUITING,
EVALUATING, SELECTING, ONBOARDING &
BUILDING GREAT TEAMS

THE DAILY COACH WAS CO-FOUNDED BY
George Raveling, Michael Lombardi, and Kimati Ramsey

The Daily Coach Press Quantity Sales Discounts
The Daily Coach Press titles are available at significant quantity discounts when purchased in bulk for client gifts, conferences, sales promotions, team building, and premiums.

For details and discount information on print formats, contact newsletter@thedaily.coach.

Copyright © 2025 The Daily Coach LLC
All rights reserved.

No part of this publication may be reproduced, stored in, or introduced into a retrieval system, or transmitted in any form or by any means (electronic, mechanical, photocopying, recording, or otherwise) without prior permission from the publisher. Requests for permission should be directed to newsletter@thedaily.coach.

Library of Congress Cataloging-in-Publication Data
Title: *Hiring: 70 Timeless Lessons and Transformational Stories on Recruiting, Evaluating, Selecting, Onboarding & Building Great Teams*

ISBN (hardcover): 979-8-9934715-0-1
ISBN (paperback): 979-8-9934715-8-7
ISBN (digital): 979-8-9934715-7-0

This book is dedicated to our dear friend and mentor, our co-founder, and our beloved "Coach," the late great George Henry Raveling.

June 27, 1937 — September 1, 2025

CONTENTS

Introduction 8

Define

Who Am I as a Leader? 12
Coachability 15
Hit The Range 17
Team of Character 19
The 4 Types of Coaches 21
Stephen Curry is Never Satisfied 24
The Knight Tapes: What Makes a Great Player Great 26
The Difference Between Good and Great 28
Sticktoitiveness: The 8 Traits of Grit 30
Wizard of Westwood 32
The Best of the Best 34
Establishing a Champion's Mindset 36
Having the Right Systems 38
The Questions on the Elevator Ride 40
Nick Saban and the 3 Flexibilities 42
The Distance Few Cross: Talent vs. Stardom 44

Attract

Bozo Explosion 48
The Power of Storytelling 50
Mastering Yourself: Lessons from a Former
Secret Service Agent 53
You're Talented. But Do You Study the Craft? 56
Jimmy Buffett, the Storyteller 59
The Years Before the Bright Lights 62
'What Could I Be Missing Here?' 64
The Value of Our Word 66
Who We Lead 68
Why We Should Be in Founder Mode 70

Evaluate

Understanding the People We Lead 74
The 7 Elements of Team Composition 77
The Truth Test: What "Good Will Hunting" Teaches
Us About Authentic Hiring 79
Why Every Leader Needs a SWOT Analysis 82
The Four P's 84
The Undercooked Steak 86
'The Numbers Stink' 88
The Rule of Thirds: Olympian Alexi Pappas on Chasing
Dreams & Embracing Crappy Days 90
The 6 Types of Genius 93
The 4 Steps of Risk Evaluation 95
Crichton, Gell-Mann Amnesia and the NFL Draft 97

Changing Minds: Three Kinds of Truth 99
'Are You About Winning?' 101

Select

The 3 Types of Underachievers 104
Soldier Vs. Scout's Mindset 107
The NFL Draft and Shoshin 109
All the Coach Wants 111
Barrels vs. Ammunition 113
Hats, Haircuts and Tattoos 115
The Problem With 'Shaping' Decisions 117
3 Rules of Simplicity 119
What Do They Know That I Don't? 121
The NFL Draft and 'Preference Falsification' 123
The Battle of Inattentional Blindness 125
Don't Be Old School 127
NFL Draft Day Decisions 129
Let's Not Anchor Our Decisions 131
NFL Vacancies and the 37 Percent Rule 133
How Biased Are Your Decisions? 135
We Must Eliminate Plan Continuation Bias 137
Bus Driver Players 139

Onboard

Take Yourself On: The Leadership Lesson
Every New Hire Needs 142
Managing Day 1 of NFL Training Camp 145

Rules for Talent	147
Effort vs. Excellence: What Really Matters	149
Level 5 Leadership: The Journey from Good to Great	151
It Ain't a Halloween Costume: The Daily Discipline of Winning	153
Taking Over a Toxic Workplace	156
How Coach K Commanded the Room	158
The 3 Major Problems With Incentivizing Talent	160
Are We Unlocking Doors for Others?	162
The Leadership Power of 'You're Allowed to Make a Mistake	164
Derek Jeter on Failure: 'Don't Let the Speed Bump Become a Roadblock	166
Winning Without Being Defined by the Win	169

INTRODUCTION

The Daily Coach was founded in 2019 by the late, great Naismith Basketball Hall of Famer "Coach" George Raveling, NFL Super Bowl–winning executive Michael Lombardi, and storyteller Kimati Ramsey.

Our mission is to improve the quality of leadership in society by honoring great leaders and great leadership in sports.

The Daily Coach is best known for our daily email, read each morning by tens of thousands of leaders, including some of the best coaches and CEOs. You can subscribe to our daily email and learn more about other opportunities to take you and your organization's leadership skills to the next level at www.thedaily.coach.

We believe leadership is one of the greatest forms of leverage. It shapes the organizations we work in, the teams we root for, and the families and communities we belong to. And in a world where so many feel isolated and disconnected, transformational leadership has never been more vital.

Why Hiring Matters

Hiring is one of the most critical leadership decisions we make.

Yet many of us are never truly taught how to evaluate character, identify alignment, or build a team culture that endures.

Hiring is a curated collection of The Daily Coach's best stories, lessons, and frameworks on recruiting, evaluating, selecting, and onboarding. Drawn from the locker rooms, boardrooms, and classrooms of some of the most respected leaders and thinkers in the world.

The Daily Coach has facilitated hundreds of conversations on leadership and team building with transformational leaders in sports and business, and more often than not, the dialogue returns to the importance of finding the right people. That's why we chose to publish this collection first.

Hiring isn't just about choosing talent. It's about vision. It's about alignment. It's about identifying the people who will elevate the culture and accelerate the mission.

Hiring serves as a compass for that process. Reminding us that selecting the right people goes far beyond checking boxes.

At The Daily Coach, we don't believe leadership is reserved for a select few. Everyone is a coach. And everyone deserves tools that help them lead with greater clarity, courage, and care.

Hiring is one of those tools.

How to Use This Book

This book is designed not only for reflection but also for action. Each chapter features one of our most impactful stories from The Daily Coach, carefully selected from the thousands of articles we've written. At the beginning of each chapter, you will find a QR code that takes you directly to the digital version of that article.

By scanning the code, you can read the story online for free and share it instantly with your team, players, colleagues, or anyone who might benefit from reading it.

We created this feature so the wisdom in these pages lives beyond the book itself. As our late co-founder George Raveling often reminded us, "Nothing in life is of any value unless you can share it with others."

The QR codes give you a simple way to revisit key lessons, spark conversation, and put ideas into practice with the people you lead. We hope *Hiring* becomes a trusted reference you return to whenever you face important decisions about growing your team.

For more ways to engage with The Daily Coach and to continue your leadership journey, visit www.thedaily.coach.

DEFINE

STORIES ON DEFINING

WHO AM I AS A LEADER?

If you visit the Green Bay Packers Hall of Fame, you'll find a replica of former head coach Vince Lombardi's office on display. The space is arranged as if Lombardi were still working there, complete with family photos displayed prominently on the credenza behind him. On the wall, plaques commemorate Lombardi's achievements as a teacher during his formative years at Red Bank Catholic High School. Lombardi took immense pride in his teaching skills, which significantly shaped his leadership style.

Similarly, national champion basketball coach Dan Hurley has always taken pride in his teaching roots. Hurley often reflects on his time at St. Benedict's Preparatory School in Newark, New Jersey, and how those experiences molded him into the elite college basketball coach he is. He has credited teaching with helping him master the art of managing a classroom, starting at St. Anthony High School, where he taught health, physical education, sex education, and driver's education, and continuing at St. Benedict's, where he worked throughout much of the 2000s.

At St. Benedict's, Hurley's responsibilities spanned far beyond teaching. He managed parent meetings, recruited talent from the inner city, and built a powerhouse basketball program. Former students describe Hurley as having an undeniable presence, a sharp sense of humor, and a unique swagger. Those early teaching days were instrumental in developing the leadership skills that define him.

Both Hurley and Lombardi used their time as teachers to refine and expand their leadership philosophies. Too often, when coaches enter their fields, they focus on strategy, fundamentals, and technique but overlook a critical question: Who am I as a leader? Teaching, with its inherent challenges and opportunities, forces individuals to confront this question and prioritize their growth as leaders.

Determining who you want to be as a leader is a vital step in your journey. It requires introspection, clarity of values, and aligning your actions with your aspirations. Here are key steps to consider:

1. **Self-Reflection and Core Values**

   Begin by reflecting on your past experiences, current challenges, and the leaders you admire. This introspection helps you define your core values and the qualities you aim to embody. Ask yourself:

   - What leadership experiences have shaped me?
   - What are my biggest leadership challenges?
   - Who are my role models, and what do I admire about them?

2. **Defining Your Leadership Compass**

   Use your reflections to create an "inner leadership compass" that guides your actions and decisions. This compass should reflect the type of leader you aspire to be. For example, you might aim to be a leader who:

   - Earns respect while delivering meaningful results
   - Demonstrates compassion and genuine care for others

- Supports team members without making assumptions
- Stands up for others and communicates effectively

3. **Balancing Aspirations and Organizational Needs**

    Effective leadership is about finding harmony between your personal aspirations and the needs of your team and organization. Consider:

    - How can I align my leadership style with organizational goals?
    - Am I fostering a culture of trust, respect, and psychological safety?
    - How can I prioritize mental health and well-being for my team?

Teaching at the high school level forces leaders to confront these foundational questions. Without clear answers, even the deepest knowledge of a game or field will fall short. Some may view Lombardi's and Hurley's teaching days as detours or delays in their careers, but in reality, the classroom was where they were forged into the extraordinary leaders they became.

COACHABILITY

Going to a prestigious college can make you more desirable in the job market.

Being highly skilled in an area can also enhance your value.

Having influential friends can help advance your career. So can hard work and dedication.

However, the most important trait any candidate can bring to the job market is "coachability."

The desire to be better and the willingness to change will always trump contacts, friends in high places, polished resumes and work ethic.

Coachability is the No. 1 trait we all need to lead, learn, and grow.

It's easy to claim we are "coachable." Maintaining coachability is the hard part.

As we get more comfortable and gain more knowledge, we often reduce our willingness to accept coaching. We move from learner to knower.

When we make this slight shift, we don't grow. We plateau our level of performance in every area of our life. We become complacent instead of committed.

Bill Campbell, in the book *The Trillion Dollar Coach,* once sat down with a young, highly successful entrepreneur, and asked: "Do you think you're coachable?"

The response was, "depends on who the coach is." Once hearing the answer, Campbell, without saying a word, walked out of the meeting. Campbell understood his ability to help this person was going to be a waste of time, because he wasn't coachable or didn't understand what it meant to be coachable.

Everyone will claim they want help, they want a mentor, or someone to offer advice along the way. Yet those are shallow words, as more often than not, saying you are coachable and being coachable are not related.

Coaching relationships evaporate because the person wanting to be coached decides they don't need coaching. They think they have all the answers. And because they are not coachable, most of those answers are to the wrong test.

As leaders we must build a coachable culture. We cannot assume everyone wants to be coached, even though their words scream "make me better." People might claim they are open to coaching, but unless they are actively seeking out coaching, they are not ready to be coached.

When Campbell left the room without saying a word, the young entrepreneur was surprised and embarrassed, causing him to react with a strong scream, "Wait! Let's talk. I'm ready." He went from being open to the idea of being coached to depending on a coach to help.

Once he shifted his mindset from depending on who the coach is to actively wanting to be coached, he moved from hearing advice to listening to advice.

Being open to coaching is wonderful, but it doesn't make you coachable. Only when you actively seek out coaching do you become coachable.

Once you make those you lead understand the difference, you will see an immediate result.

HIT THE RANGE

Shane Lowry's victory at the Open Championship on his home soil was a moment of national pride. All of Ireland beamed as Lowry fought off challenging weather on the final day and held onto his commanding lead. Winning a Major is an extraordinary individual achievement, and watching Lowry's face burst with pride as he walked up the eighteenth hole, waving to the fans, was the culmination of years of effort.

Hard work, diligence, competitive spirit, talent, mental toughness, and most of all, a willingness to be honest about every part of his game were written all over his bearded face.

Professional golfers are no different from coaches, leaders, or anyone striving for excellence. They carry fourteen clubs to every event, and how they use those clubs determines their success. They practice each one, never ignoring the weaker clubs or relying only on their favorites. They know their weaknesses, and they put in hours on the range to improve both strengths and shortcomings. After a bad round, a good round, or an average one, they return to the range. For them to compete, they must constantly refine every club.

You also carry at least fourteen clubs in your coaching or leadership bag. Do you use them all every day? Do you find ways to improve? Do you avoid the "bad clubs" and only lean on your strengths? Most importantly, do you know which areas need growth? Take time today to write down the tools you possess as a coach or leader, then give yourself an honest assessment. It might be more than fourteen, it might be fewer. The point isn't perfection in a single day but steady, daily improvement. Like a golfer, hit the range and work on those areas that need sharpening through reading, learning, and reflection.

It's striking how many coaches commit to physical workouts, which are vital, yet claim they don't have time to read. Your mind, just like your body, needs disciplined training. Start a mental fitness plan the same way you would a physical one: begin slowly, build consistency, and expand over time. Enhancing intellect is as important as conditioning the body. If someone asks what you're reading, tell them you're training your mind. Soon, those around you will start reading too.

Every season, on the first day of practice, coaches stand before their teams and demand improvement. They want growth, even if it's just one percent more. That same expectation must apply to leaders themselves. Work your craft. Know your strengths. Confront your weaknesses. Then hit the range and commit to small daily gains.

Before long, you'll have your own walk up eighteen, just like Shane Lowry.

TEAM OF CHARACTER

On September 12, 1970, USC played the University of Alabama at Birmingham's Legion Field. It was the first time an integrated team from outside the state came to Alabama to face one of the last all-white squads in the country. The game is often credited with changing college football, yet it wasn't a single game that brought reform. It was the lifelong work of one man behind the scenes.

Three hundred miles southeast of Birmingham, in Tallahassee, Florida, Jake Gaither was quietly building a powerhouse at Florida A&M University. The son of a preacher, Gaither chose to impact lives not from a pulpit but from the sidelines, as a high school and college football coach.

During World War II, Florida A&M's head coach, Bill Bell, left his post to serve in the war. The university paused its football program for a season. Searching for a successor, President William H. Gray Jr. turned to Jake Gaither, then an assistant on Bell's staff who had survived a brain tumor just three years earlier. Gaither took over in 1945 and went on to become one of only eighty-nine coaches in history to record more than 200 college wins.

By the late 1950s, Gaither had instituted an annual coaching clinic that drew some of the biggest names in sports. Alabama's Paul "Bear" Bryant, Arkansas' Frank Broyles, Texas' Darrell Royal, Ohio State's Woody Hayes, and Kentucky's Adolph "The Baron" Rupp were among the many who came to teach and learn. These clinics weren't just about X's and O's. They were about the game of life.

Gaither used learning as a bridge to confront racial inequality in a deeply divided South. He refused to let barriers stop him from being a difference-maker. His clinics gave Florida A&M stature far beyond the Black College realm and helped propel the program into the American sports mainstream. Soon, Florida A&M and other HBCUs were competing against predominantly white programs in the late 1960s and early 1970s, laying the groundwork for NCAA and NAIA membership across sports.

Gaither's moral courage outshone even his 200 wins. Robert F. Kennedy, in his "Day of Affirmation" speech in South Africa, said, "Moral courage is a rarer commodity than bravery in battle or great intelligence. Yet it is the one essential, vital quality for those who seek to change a world that yields most painfully to change."

Though change was painful, Coach Gaither transformed college football. He used education and continuous learning as a bridge, forging friendships and experiences that challenged people to look beyond the obvious and beneath the surface.

Gaither once declared, "I run into so many people who have no deep sense of morals, people who've got a price tag on them, who'd sell their soul. I want to find the man who has no price tag on him. I'm not for sale."

Don't be a person for sale. And don't allow people into your organization who wear a price tag.

Build a team of character, not characters. Be like Coach Gaither.

THE 4 TYPES OF COACHES

College football has become a massive business in America, with money flowing into conferences through lucrative TVcontracts. This revenue has bolstered countless athletic programs across the country.

College players are no longer considered amateurs, as they can now be legally compensated for their impact on the field. Coaches' salaries have risen dramatically as well, and with that increase have come heightened expectations from fan bases. As a result, coaching turnover is at an all-time high.

When a coaching search begins, schools hunt for the next Nick Saban or Kirby Smart, leaders who have dominated the college landscape. But few truly understand what makes these coaches effective; they simply want their success.

In reality, schools often default to hiring coaches who fit into three categories:

The Schemer
This coach has demonstrated proficiency and expertise in a specific area of the game. Schools that hire the "Schemer" believe this will vault them into the winner's circle. But schemes never win by themselves. They only help.

The Caretaker
This coach provides some cachet and brand power, relying on hiring a strong staff for him to oversee rather than direct. He cannot solve problems other than by firing and hiring another expert.

The Recruiter
This coach has deep connections with high schools and can connect personally with players, giving the program access to top talent.

What's missing in most searches, both in college and the pros, is the Strategist. This is the leader capable of handling the three elements above, and far more. The Strategist can anticipate problems, ask the right questions, and build something sustainable.

The Strategist cares about both the present and the near future. They understand the art of team building, focus on helping staff members improve their skill sets, and anchor their work in core beliefs that adapt to current realities.

The Strategist is a leader, not a manager. Remember the difference: Leaders do the right thing. Managers do things right. The three other types are essentially managers. When conditions are less than perfect, their margin of error grows, and another coaching search begins.

After firing a coach, schools often hire someone strong in the area where the former coach was weakest. This pattern is a clear sign the school doesn't understand its true problems. The perceived flaws of the last coach may not be the real cause of the program's decline.

Without a strategist, no program can achieve consistent success. Without deliberately searching for a strategist, universities and NFL teams will continue the cycle of hiring and firing, never moving closer to solving their underlying issues.

And if the organization hires one of the three manager types, who then becomes the strategist? The athletic director? The top donor? The fans? The media? The alumni? The answer: all of the above, which is exactly why teams change coaches so frequently.

Coaches need to spend less time buried in schemes and more time developing a full understanding of the game, not just how to design plays, but how to shape organizations. Once a coach moves beyond the narrow confines of

DEFINE

schemer, caretaker, or recruiter and steps into the strategist's role, the program begins to grow in every area.

Coaches constantly ask their players to grow their skill sets and improve daily. The same advice applies to them.

Become a strategist, not a schemer.

STEPHEN CURRY IS NEVER SATISFIED

The road to stardom for NBA superstar Stephen Curry wasn't easy. Many thought he would never get a chance. Curry's father, Dell Curry, once walked through an airport and ran into his son's youth coach, who told him, "Your son's going to make a lot of money from this game one day." Dell thought he meant overseas. Stephen was short, frail, and released his shot below his waist, meaning he would get blocked once he competed against bigger and stronger players. At that point, there was nothing elite about his skill set.

"I don't even remember seeing him (during his college recruitment process). I do know when I did see him later, I thought, 'Man, he is little,'" former North Carolina coach Roy Williams said.

Dell wasn't hard on his son or negative. As a former NBA player himself, he knew what it took to play in the league. And at that moment, he hadn't seen Stephen demonstrate those skills. Since Stephen was a below-average athlete for that level, he needed to alter his game to rise above his weaknesses. Curry changed his shot mechanics, built the strength to have unlimited range, and worked relentlessly on his conditioning to ensure he would never get tired during a game.

When you watch him play, you might think he's a natural talent. In reality, the skills he displays are the product of countless hours working to perfect his craft.

Curry has that unique trait all extremely talented people share: he behaves as if he doesn't have talent. He carries an overachiever's mentality, ignoring the praises, knowing the road to achievement comes only from doing the work, every single day. He cannot take a day off for fear his edge will vanish. He shows up daily, believing that unless he gives everything he has, he will fail. This is not an act, but a mindset forever ingrained by past struggles.

Isn't it interesting that two of the greatest athletes of their generation, Tom Brady and Stephen Curry, were overlooked coming out of high school? Neither was supposed to have a great professional career. Yet both have achieved greatness, and both continued to work as if they hadn't won anything. Their relentless fuel comes from the sting of their past failures.

People with this quality are never satisfied with yesterday's results. They only know they must work before the competition begins. Curry didn't inherit a "talent gene" from his father. What he received instead was the never satisfied gene, which, in the end, is often far more valuable.

THE KNIGHT TAPES: WHAT MAKES A GREAT PLAYER GREAT

In 1971, Indiana University hired Robert Montgomery Knight as head coach from the United States Military Academy. Over nearly three decades, Knight's Hoosier teams won 662 games, including twenty-two seasons of 20 or more wins, while losing 239, a .735 overall winning percentage.

In 24 NCAA tournament appearances at Indiana, Knight's teams won 42 of 63 games (.667), capturing national titles in 1976, 1981, and 1987, while reaching the semifinals in 1973 and 1992. Knight built one of the most successful programs in college basketball, and his lessons on coaching remain applicable in any sport or organization.

A friend of The Daily Coach shared a video from the early 1980s of Knight explaining what makes a great basketball player. Seated in his team's room with a video machine in front of him, Knight spoke plainly to his audience. He outlined five critical points he demanded from the players he recruited and coached. Before listing them, he emphasized that talent was not his most important criterion. For Knight, thinking about the game and understanding its nuances always outweighed sheer ability. Smart players, he believed, bring more value than raw talent.

Coach Knight's Five Rules

1. **Play to your potential.** There can be no inconsistency. Players must perform at the same high level against all opponents and deliver steady results each outing.
2. **Know your strengths and weaknesses.** Great players understand both. They continue to work on their strengths while devoting extra effort to their weaknesses. They never play outside of their strong points,

and they never allow opponents to expose their shortcomings.

3. **Know your teammates.** Great players understand the strengths and weaknesses of their teammates as well as their own. They communicate effectively, ensuring the team plays in the way that best serves everyone. The focus is always on how the team can win, not on personal statistics.

4. **Understand how to avoid losing.** Every sport has fundamentals that, if neglected, lead to defeat. Knight insisted his players master the basics and know the common ways teams lose before they could ever learn how to win. Drill the fundamentals daily.

5. **See and look. Hear and listen.** Knight believed these words had to work together. Everyone looks at the game, but not everyone sees the details. Everyone hears instruction, but not everyone listens. Great players do both.

Knight also reminded his audience that great teams keep things simple. They focus on clarity, execution, and fundamentals. Success, he believed, always comes back to simplicity and discipline.

With much appreciation, we reviewed Coach Knight's timeless tape. His five rules are as relevant today as when he first delivered them, and we hope you can apply them to your own teams and organizations.

THE DIFFERENCE BETWEEN GOOD AND GREAT

We as leaders evaluate talent every day, so it's imperative that we understand the true meaning of great.

Good players play well some of the time. Great players play great all of the time. The level of competition is the clearest and most vital indication. The higher the stakes, the better great players perform. They cannot be taken out. Understanding the level of competition is the best way to appreciate the difference between good and great.

Great players work the hardest. They are never satisfied. They are fueled by the desire to achieve and driven by curiosity to improve. As Robert Hughes once said, "The greater the artist, the greater the doubt. Perfect confidence is granted to the less talented as a consolation prize."

Great players always want to do more. Good players feel they have done all they can.

Killer Instincts, Players and Staff

Success can be like a martini, it can make everyone delusional, leading to the belief that there is no need to go the extra mile. "We got this" becomes the mantra instead of "We have earned nothing."

With championship-level teams, achievements are rarely mentioned. The focus is always on what lies ahead. What can we do tomorrow? How can we get better? These become the mission statements for the organization. And there is always someone, a coach, a captain, a leader, who drives the team to fight off the natural instinct of contentment.

Mental Toughness

To compete at a championship level, we must build both mental and physical toughness. True toughness means proving it daily, on and off the field.

What sets disciplined people apart?

- The capacity to get past distractions
- The willingness to condition both mind and body for the task at hand
- The ability to maintain poise when those around them are losing theirs

Boxer Joe Lipsey was once a 17:1 underdog fighting Marvin Hagler. Lipsey dominated the first three rounds, but Hagler eventually sent him to the hospital with a single blow in the fourth. After the fight, Lipsey's trainer asked, "Joe, what happened?"

"I gave him my best shot at the end of round 3," Lipsey replied, "and it didn't even faze him."

Hagler's mental toughness, his ability to absorb Lipsey's best and keep coming forward, ultimately broke his opponent.

So when you're competing and you get beaten on a play, what are you conveying? When you get back up, what is your body language exhibiting?

Nick Saban put it best: *"To wear a player down, everybody wants to play hard in the beginning of the game. It takes a long time to wear a player down, so you have to have a tremendous amount of mental toughness to be able to do that, to sustain it yourself."*

STICKTOITIVENESS: THE 8 TRAITS OF GRIT

> *"Learning to stick to something is a life skill that we all have to develop."*
> — **Angela Duckworth**

For those who went to Catholic school, you might remember the nuns telling you and your peers to develop "sticktoitiveness." Nuns urged students to make sure "sticktoitiveness" went into each homework assignment, and preached the word as if it were written in the Bible. The term "sticktoitiveness" was a daily call to action for them to educate and inspire excellence and perseverance. They wanted everyone to stay the course, to not give up, and to finish everything once started. The nuns were instilling a mindset to never allow the workload or other obstacles to interfere with accomplishing a task. The teachings of "sticktoitiveness" empowered students to develop a relentless spirit while always staying gritty.

Pioneering psychologist Angela Duckworth specializes in studying grit and self-control. Her first book, *Grit: The Power of Passion and Perseverance*, was published in 2016 and featured on *The New York Times* bestseller list for several weeks.

Duckworth has found "Grit" to be a common factor in the high-achievers she has studied. Her work suggests that grit is unrelated to intelligence but highly related to conscientiousness. Duckworth, like the nuns, believes grit is essential for everyone; however, it works best when teaching adolescents.

Duckworth's studies show: when young children develop conscientious behavioral traits as core habits, they can become high achievers. So, the Catholic nuns, according to Duckworth, were not wrong after all.

So what are the traits Angela Duckworth believes all "gritty" people possess?

- Gritty people focus on high-level pursuits but are flexible on low-level goals.
- Gritty people know the "Why" behind everything they do.
- Gritty people live life as a marathon, not a sprint.
- Gritty people are stubborn, not stupid.
- Gritty people work hard but work only with great focus and purpose.
- Gritty people view setbacks as comeback opportunities.
- Gritty people avoid distractions.
- Gritty people never feel anxious or ashamed in the face of adversity. They look for ways to improve and get better.

Duckworth believes that effort times talent equals skill, and skill times effort equals achievement. Cultivating a mindset of grit while practicing these eight traits can make all the difference in our personal and professional lives.

Angela Duckworth also believes hope plays an important role. She writes, "Grit depends on a different kind of hope. It rests on the expectation that our own efforts can improve our future."

Based on Duckworth's trailblazing research, we can improve our future with grit. There is no better time to start than now.

WIZARD OF WESTWOOD

How could we have *The Daily Coach* without mentioning the late, great UCLA basketball coach John Wooden and everything he mastered when it came to teaching?

Wooden's principles on teaching, leading, and serving have withstood the test of time, regardless of sport, gender, or generation.

One of the best Wooden stories ever told is a powerful reminder for all coaches, teachers, leaders, and change agents.

Coach Wooden was always generous with his time. If young coaches invested the energy and resources to learn from the Wizard of Westwood, he would grant them an audience. On one occasion, he met with a first-time head coach. They spoke for hours, and the young coach filled two notebooks with the wisdom Wooden shared.

At the end of the meeting, Wooden thanked the coach and said:

"I am thrilled we had a chance to bond today. It was a delightful time. But you could have saved your school money and yourself time, because out of all those pages of notes, there are only three things that matter."

1. Define and recruit talent that fits your system.
2. Make sure you always recruit players who put the team ahead of themselves.
3. Don't try to become a coaching genius or guru. Understand the variables a player must perform and practice simplicity with constant repetition.

Wooden saw himself as a teacher first. He worked tirelessly on the finer details of the game. His ego never got in the way of being a servant leader or of winning with grace. And he understood the value of preparation.

When preparing for practice, he told his secretary: "Unless there was an earthquake, I am not to be bothered by anyone."

Read that again. He never allowed interruptions during preparation. Do you? Is your phone within reach? Can anyone pull you away in the middle of a strategy meeting? If so, it's time to rethink your preparation process, even when planning your day. Eliminate distractions and protect that sacred time.

Wooden's method of simplicity with constant repetition allowed him to craft specific game plans without clutter. He never needed a massive play sheet filled with endless calls, just a rolled-up piece of paper. From the outside, his coaching seemed complex. But for his players and staff, it was simple, clear, and repeatable.

That's the paradox of great teachers: they appear simple, but their mastery of detail makes them profound.

So today, streamline what you want from your employees, students, or players. Spend more time coaching the details with constant reps.

The rewards, as Wooden showed us, will be great.

THE BEST OF THE BEST

Hall of Fame coach Bill Belichick says, *"Talent will determine the floor. Character will determine the ceiling."*

Talent matters for every team. But character, built on complete trust, is what allows people to grow, improve, and truly belong.

Trustworthiness is always the foundation when evaluating character. Understanding character begins and ends with assessing a person's ability to be trusted.

Simon Sinek, author of *Start With Why*, *Leaders Eat Last*, and *The Infinite Game*, has devoted much of his work to exploring what makes great teams thrive. In his research on the Navy SEALs' selection process, he uncovered powerful lessons about how trust outweighs talent at the highest levels.

SEAL Team 6 represents the best of the best. Passing BUD/S training is already an extraordinary feat, but being invited to join SEAL Team 6 borders on the impossible. Sinek discovered that their selection criteria revealed a simple but profound truth: they would rather have someone less talented but completely trusted than the most talented candidate whose trustworthiness was in question.

As one SEAL put it: "I may trust you with my life, but do I trust you with my money or my wife?"

Here are three reasons why they value trust over talent:

1. **Trust must be universal.** If trust doesn't extend to every area of life, it can't be fully counted on in the most critical ones. A person who bends the rules in one area will eventually erode confidence everywhere. On a team where unity is survival, that's unacceptable.

2. **Trust increases speed.** High trust accelerates communication. With trust, people act quickly, without second-guessing motives or strategies. Low trust, however, slows everything down. Time and energy are wasted convincing others of the plan, and even then, buy-in is incomplete. In high-stakes environments, there's no margin for hesitation.

3. **Pressure reveals trustworthiness.** When pressure rises, character is exposed. Cracks hidden under calm conditions become clear when responsibilities grow or adversity hits. Trustworthiness must hold firm in the toughest moments, not just the easy ones.

So how do we define trust when selecting our team members?

Remember: past performance will always point toward future behavior. When hiring or building teams, spend more time evaluating character than talent.

Talent may set the floor, but trust and character will always determine the ceiling.

ESTABLISHING A CHAMPION'S MINDSET

It has become a "must-watch" event for NFL fans worldwide during the off-season.

Former college players dressed in T-shirts and shorts run the forties, vertical jump, broad jump, and perform other assorted drills to showcase their athletic prowess. And when a player does something impressive, like run a fast 40 or jump like Superman, the results go viral, and the player's value rises in the draft.

Though the drills don't necessarily have anything to do with the game of football, the results are powerful.

What cannot be tested or evaluated during the players' time at the NFL Draft Combine is their heart and their champion's mindset, something Dr. Jim Afremow has spent a lifetime studying and teaching.

Afremow has written an incredible book on how we as athletes, leaders, teachers, and parents can develop a "Champion's Mindset," emphasizing that before we can perform like a champion, we must remove self-doubt and think like one.

For Afremow, being the best centers on your mindset before any work occurs. Preparing your mind to be the best starts with B.E.S.T.

B. Belief
When you believe you can become a champion, your training is champion-like. What Afremow suggests to the athletes he trains is to believe they finished second in the last event, fuel the belief with needing to raise your level ever so slightly.

E. Enjoyment
When Jesse Owens won four gold medals in Nazi Germany at the 1936 Olympics, he focused on the joy around

him, not the hate. He said "find the good, it's all around." We gain more enjoyment when we enjoy the process and look forward to working. Embrace the work. Love it, and with enjoyment comes progress.

S. Self Talk
We hate having ants in our homes, and we should never have ants on our minds. ANTS (Automatic Negative Thoughts) create doubt, they create uncertainty, and the quicker we remove them, the better we prepare.

T. Toughness
For Afremow, being mentally tough is critical to having the mindset of a champion. And being mentally tough means moving on from a mistake while remaining positive and proactive.

Having great athletic talent is a wonderful skill, but without a champion's mindset, it can never reach its full potential.

A player with a fast forty is great. A player with a champion's mindset is better.

HAVING THE RIGHT SYSTEMS

In 2023, Carolina Panthers owner David Tepper defended his hasty decisions regarding the coaches of both his football and soccer teams.

With Frank Reich being the third head coach dismissed under his ownership, Tepper was asked if he needed to re-evaluate his own approach moving forward.

"Look, things are constantly evolving, and they'll continue to evolve," he told Joe Person of *The Athletic*. "Tryin' to make things better is what you always try to do. Obviously, that record is not good enough. There's no hiding it, it is what it is, like everything in this sport. Everything's left on the field, everybody knows what it is every week. That record's that record. And, like I said, it's not good enough. We're gonna self-reflect and make it better."

He added: "I would like to have somebody here as coach for 20 or 30 years. I would like to have somebody who is young enough that they would say the eulogy at my funeral in 30 years. O.K., maybe it's 40 years, I hope."

Tepper's words reveal a fundamental misunderstanding of what it takes to build a championship organization. One man doesn't last forty years. Sustained success comes only when systems and processes are in place. Tepper doesn't need one man, he needs an operating system.

The "lone star" model of hiring in the NFL has proven to be a failure. With nearly one-third of head coaches fired each year, the problem is rarely the hire itself. It's the organization. In a knowledge-driven industry, one of the most important risks leaders must manage is the risk of weak team building. A strong team is not one where a single person disproportionately influences the outcome, that's closer to a dictatorship. While champions and leaders are valuable, business continuity requires structures and systems.

Gino Wickman, author of *Traction: Get a Grip on Your Business*, writes: "All successful organizations and companies have a system, a system that they flow, throughout the organization."

Wickman calls this a solution-oriented environment: "When everyone follows their process, it's much easier for managers to manage, to troubleshoot, identify and solve issues, and therefore grow the business. The clear lines enable you to let go and gain more control."

The ability to identify and solve problems as they arise is the lifeblood of organizational traction. Systems make problem-solving easier, leaders more effective, and organizations more successful. Tepper thinks he needs a coach to develop his quarterback. But even if the next coach succeeds in that task, another challenge will inevitably arise. Without systems, one solved problem only gives way to another.

Tepper is searching for the impossible, a single person who can fulfill every need. But what he actually needs is clarity: to identify his vision for the Panthers, surround himself with people who share that vision, remain open-minded and growth-oriented, and build the organization from the inside out, not the outside in.

Without a system, without standards, Tepper will never find the person who will stand at his funeral delivering those kinds of words.

THE QUESTIONS ON THE ELEVATOR RIDE

Albert Einstein once said his best ideas came when he was either on a walk or in the shower.

Einstein believed that when his mind was completely relaxed, insights would spring into his head that helped him solve the problems dominating his life.

As leaders, we're always searching for information about our organizations from those on the ground level. And to create true vertical alignment, there must be a clear flow from bottom to top, not simply the other way around.

A simple elevator ride can be one of the best places to gather that information. Mingling with people during a short trip can provide surprising clarity about how to improve our ability to lead.

When in an elevator with people on your right and left, ask these three questions:

- What do you do?
- What is the strategy of the organization?
- How does what you do support the strategy?

Duke Ellington once said, "I don't need more time; I need a deadline."

An elevator ride provides the perfect time restriction to elicit answers. If a leader asks the right questions, even those brief responses can offer tremendous insight. The more specific the question, the more detailed the answer.

If you ask, "Do you like your job?" a simple "Yes" ends the conversation. But if you reframe it as, "What are three reasons besides salary that you like your job?" the answers become far more revealing.

Why wouldn't this work outside the elevator? Because when someone is surrounded by peers, honesty is harder to come by. The elevator setting creates an environment where compliance drops, thoughtfulness rises, and answers are harder to fudge, which gives leaders valuable insight into whether the organization is truly vertically aligned.

Remember: building a great culture requires both horizontal and vertical alignment. A team cannot be aligned if those on the ground level don't understand the strategy or their role in the bigger picture.

Don't just ride the elevator. Use it as an opportunity to learn about your team.

NICK SABAN AND THE 3 FLEXIBILITIES

There is a great clip of Nick Saban discussing how he had to adapt his coaching to pro football. Saban admits he could no longer remain status quo by only playing the athletes who adhered strictly to his coaching style and teachings. He realized he needed to broaden his thinking, to change, and to become willing to coach "inside-out," not "outside-in."

Coaching "outside-in" means forcing players to adapt to your methods. Coaching "inside-out" means adapting your methods to the players' skill sets. Coaches who teach inside-out determine their players' strengths and weaknesses and plan accordingly, never asking someone to do something outside their capacity.

Does this mean Saban abandoned his philosophy of how to win the game? No chance. Does this mean he stopped demanding from his players? No chance. All Saban did was adapt. His

core foundation of leadership and the principles of his program never changed.

He simply employed three forms of flexibility that allowed him to thrive in a new environment.

1. **Cognitive Flexibility.** The ability to use different thinking strategies and mental frameworks. Cognitive flexibility requires nimble, divergent thinking, an openness to developing new approaches, and the ability to see and leverage new connections. Saban had to let go of one of his long-held teaching beliefs and embrace a new approach.
2. **Emotional Flexibility.** The ability to vary one's approach to managing emotions, both your own and others'. Leaders with emotional flexibility adapt their style

depending on the situation. In Saban's case, the enormous salaries of professional players forced him to shift emotionally. As he once told Art Modell: "None of them are worth it, but they can help."

3. **Dispositional Flexibility.** The ability to remain optimistic while still being realistic. Dispositionally flexible leaders see change as an opportunity rather than as a threat. Saban's awareness of the need to adapt gave him the dispositional flexibility to embrace new circumstances without abandoning his foundation.

We all face an ever-changing world. Technology, combined with generational shifts, makes it harder than ever to lead the same way we always have. But don't confuse adaptability with abandoning your philosophy.

Work on these three areas of flexibility, cognitive, emotional, and dispositional, and you'll position yourself to lead with the same adaptability that has defined Nick Saban's success.

THE DISTANCE FEW CROSS: TALENT VS. STARDOM

Tom Brady gave an extensive interview on the evolution of how to properly evaluate the professional quarterbacking position in the NFL.

Using himself as the example, Brady went into extensive detail helping people understand TALENT wasn't the key component. According to Brady, having talent gives a player the opportunity to compete for a job.

Having proper training, teaching, and development can turn a talented player into a star player, only if the player can take the lessons from the classroom to the game field.

Brady wasn't viewed as a talented player when he was the 199th pick overall in the NFL draft. His college career was sporadic, with flashes of brilliance when he was allowed to enter the game. He had a constant battle with another, more high-profile player, often resulting in Brady being forced to take a lesser role, thus hiding his overall skills for the position. Brady wasn't viewed as a great athlete or someone with a rocket for an arm, and his lack of commanding a consistent starting role forced NFL scouts to miss his greatest quality, the ability to navigate the hardest terrain facing most athletes: moving from talent to stardom.

Moving from being a talent to being a star is arduous, requiring immersing yourself in total commitment, which Brady learned as the Patriots filled his brain with knowledge, training him to play at the highest level. This conduit allowed Brady to display his talents, assuring his coaches he had the necessary skills. Then Brady, being the ultimate competitor, moved from a talented player to becoming a star in less than three years. Everyone wondered how. Few know what is needed to move from talent to star.

The underlying theme to Brady's message isn't in the evaluation of the quarterback, rather for us to learn the difference between talent and stardom. As leaders, we must educate our talent on the distance required to reach the sacred place, ignoring the noise from the outside that is quick to anoint everyone as a star. We must demonstrate the sacrifices required to reach stardom. Talent is a gift from God, whereas stardom is the consistent application of talent toward winning.

The business and sports world are filled with talented workers. Talent is commonplace and, in some venues like professional sports, talent will receive the highest level of compensation along with praise. It was easy for the Patriots, as Brady visualizes himself as an overachiever who needs to outwork everyone every day. For most leaders, it's easy to recognize talent within each organization. What becomes hard is getting everyone to cross the long bridge. Because stardom is a small club, we must recognize some will resist the requirements, despite our efforts.

Talent is an essential quality for any organization to employ. Leaders spending time developing talent is what can hopefully cover the distance to stardom.

The bridge to stardom requires four non-negotiable qualities:

- Stars always have a high level of consistent performance against anyone.
- Stars must have an impact on the outcome of winning.
- Stars never care about individual awards.
- Stars make everyone on the team perform at a higher level.

If a talent doesn't do those four items every time, they are not a star.

They will remain a talent, someone who can garner attention but never the ultimate prize.

Brady's fingers are lined with championship rings. The distance he traveled and continues to travel, regardless of career stage, is a grueling process. He knows no other way, just as Kobe Bryant and Michael Jordan did during their careers. Not everyone can, which is why as leaders we must recognize the two distinctions.

As leaders, we must ask our talent if they want to reach stardom. If they say yes, prepare them for the long journey.

ATTRACT

STORIES ON ATTRACTING

BOZO EXPLOSION

When building a workforce, many of us believe there's a sense of urgency to make hiring decisions. Speed takes over, and filling vacant spots within the company becomes the priority. The panic caused by rushing to judgment convinces us that getting workers up and running is more important than getting the right workers.

But more people never equates to more efficient and effective production. Guy Kawasaki, formerly of Apple and Google and the author of several books, calls this the "Bozo Explosion."

The Bozo Explosion, Kawasaki explains, happens after an organization achieves success. He describes the signs like this:

- The CEO's administrator has an administrator.
- The success of a competitor upsets you more than the loss of a customer.
- The most popular words in the company are "partner" and "strategic."
- Management hosts two-day offsites at the Ritz-Carlton to "foster communication" and craft a mission statement.
- The front desk gets better looking, and less competent.

Who wants to work for that kind of organization, team, or culture?

The principle of "hire slow, fire fast" is the best practice for assembling a strong team, and it helps prevent the Bozo Explosion from taking hold. It might sound harsh to talk about hiring and firing, but having the wrong people in jobs is just as painful for them as it is for the company. Wrong hires cut both ways.

Taking time in the hiring process gives leaders the opportunity to understand the job description, the expectations, and, most importantly, how the employee will be developed. No new hire is a "ready-made" professional. Always ask: "Once we hire this person, how will we make them better?"

Stanford University has long practiced a version of "hire slow, fire fast" in its admissions. The admissions office vets prospective students with multiple layers of holistic review. Once admitted, Stanford invests heavily to ensure students complete their education. They make entry difficult, but once someone is in, they double down on development. And if something goes wrong, they address it quickly.

Building a workforce takes time. Spend that time understanding what role each hire will play. Clarify the job, define how you'll develop the talent, and be precise about the criteria required for success.

Remember: less is often more. Simplicity is key.

THE POWER OF STORYTELLING

Throughout history, stories have played a profound role in shaping our experiences and the way we view the world. They are the cherished fabric of our belief systems that connects our lessons, memories and self-discovery. Many times, though, emotionally rich stories that have the power to change the way we think, behave and lead go unheard and unacknowledged.

For instance, take the life and legacy of Mary W. Jackson, who became the first African-American female engineer at NASA in 1958. NASA later named the agency's headquarters in Washington, D.C., after her. Jackson successfully overcame the sweltering barriers of segregation, inequality, racial terror, and gender bias to become a professional aerospace engineer and a leader in ensuring equal opportunities for future generations and women of color in the field of engineering and technology.

But you see, the trailblazing genius and courageous acts of Mary W. Jackson went untold in the public eye for decades before catching widespread national attention through Margot Lee Shetterly's book *Hidden Figures: The American Dream and the Untold Story of the Black Women Mathematicians Who Helped Win the Space Race*.

The book, later adapted into a motion picture, captured the groundbreaking performance of Jackson and her three African-American female colleagues: Katherine Johnson, Dorothy Vaughan, and Christine Darden. They each served as the brains within NASA's West Area Computing Unit and behind one of the most significant space operations in history.

As leaders, coaches, and educators, we must examine the stories we have told to date and reflect on the stories we will express with high energy and purpose as we go forward. Too often, we get blindsided into repeating the same adage of others without customizing our approach and delivery for our teams. Every day, we have a unique opportunity not just to make a statement but to actually communicate a message.

Messages tell stories that resonate with the listeners. They are a commitment that builds a bridge of credibility, authenticity, trust, buy-in and stay-in.

While compelling leadership storytelling helps clarify the vision and mission of our culture, while also addressing challenges and driving organizational change, stories also humanize our interaction, thus providing moments for collective growth and discovery. Remember, people don't care how much you know until they know how much you care. Storytelling will allow you to get to the hearts and minds of those you lead.

The stories we tell reflect the awareness and insights of ourselves and of our environments. Recognize that moments of uncertainty can be influential teachers. Stories of collaboration, while using the words "WE" and "US," must continue to be told. We must allow our teams to see every moment in history as a cry for collaboration that we pull through together.

The stories we tell should frame organizational and societal problems as opportunities for exponential growth and movement forward.

So take time to understand your story and the paths others have walked to get to where they are. Each of us has a story waiting to be told. It is our responsibility as leaders, positive difference-makers, and change agents to never stop learning, unlearning, and re-learning. This daily action positions us to uncover the plethora of hidden figures whose stories remain untold.

Their experiences can become the framework we use to lead, coach, teach, empower, and inspire our teams to new levels of high performance and excellence even in times of uncertainty.

But we must put in the work first to discover these transformative narratives.

MASTERING YOURSELF: LESSONS FROM A FORMER SECRET SERVICE AGENT

In today's world of relentless demands and constant change, the ability to lead with clarity, conviction, presence, and resilience is more important than ever. Few understand this better than Evy Poumpouras, a former U.S. Secret Service Special Agent who has protected some of the world's most powerful leaders. Trained in reading people, detecting deception, and facing danger head-on, Poumpouras has honed expertise that extends beyond security into the psychology of leadership and influence.

As the bestselling author of *Becoming Bulletproof: Life Lessons from a Secret Service Agent* and co-host of Bravo's *Spy Games*, Poumpouras shared her insights on *The Diary of a CEO* podcast with Steven Bartlett. She spoke about the pitfalls of being easily offended, the danger of relying on others' opinions, and the body language mistake that weakens presence. But perhaps her most compelling takeaway was this:

"The biggest struggle people face isn't the world around them, it's themselves."

Poumpouras explained that we are often our own greatest obstacles. We sabotage progress, rationalize poor decisions, and downplay our weaknesses while inflating our strengths. Research supports this: many in the Western world minimize their faults while exaggerating their positive attributes, leading to a lack of accountability and, ultimately, a loss of control over their lives.

While external challenges and bad actors exist, Poumpouras emphasizes that personal transformation starts with the relationship we build with ourselves, our mindset, our discipline, and our decision-making. To become truly adaptable in these ever-changing times, leaders must adopt a mindset of greater ownership, intentionality in decisions and reactions, and a focused commitment to service and impact.

From her experiences in high-stakes environments, Poumpouras shares six foundational creeds that can empower leaders, coaches, executives, and high performers on their journey of leadership and personal mastery:

- **Speak with conviction.** It's not what you say, but how you say it. If you don't believe in your words, no one else will. Own what you say.
- **Respect is a gift.** If someone wants to give it, they will. If they don't, they won't. Stop chasing it. The respect you desire starts within.
- **Master the art of silence.** The person who speaks the least has the most power in the conversation. The more you speak, the less you learn and the more you reveal.
- **Motivation is an illusion.** It's fickle, fleeting, unreliable. If you wait for motivation, you'll accomplish little. Motivation leads to mediocrity. Discipline is the driver.
- **Words are like currency.** When you talk just to talk, you're passing dollar bills. When you speak with value, you're dropping hundreds.
- **Serve something greater than yourself.** Help others. Be a champion for humanity. Your time here is temporary, leave the world better than you found it.

At any given moment, some plans may be on track while others drift. The real question is: Where are you truly showing up for yourself and for those you lead?

- Which of these creeds are you already living with consistency?

- Which ones need greater attention and intentional action?
- Where might you be making excuses instead of taking ownership?

In a world full of distraction, information, and noise, we have a unique opportunity to turn inward, to focus on the most important project of all: ourselves. True transformation begins within. By cultivating discipline, clarity, and self-connection, we lay the foundation for lasting growth and meaningful impact on those we have the privilege of leading and caring for.

So, pause. Reflect. Breathe. Check in with yourself. Acknowledge what is, and if needed, make a small adjustment you can consistently commit to as you move toward what could be.

And as you step forward with purpose, remember: great leaders aren't just made, they're built, one day and one decision at a time.

YOU'RE TALENTED. BUT DO YOU STUDY THE CRAFT?

In every arena, whether it's sports, business, education, or leadership, a familiar question always resurfaces: What separates the good from the great?

It's a timeless question. One that transcends technological advances and industry trends. At its heart, it isn't about skill sets or strategy, it's about mindset, character, and the spirit of human potential.

Renowned speaker and former athlete Inky Johnson shared a powerful story about the late Hall of Famer Kobe Bryant and his evolution under the great coach Phil Jackson.

"I was studying and watching Phil talk about Kobe and how talented and skillful he was, and then he said it turned him into a different player when he started to learn the nuances of the game, and he studied it differently. The greatest players don't just manipulate the game with their talent. The greatest manipulate the game with their mind," Johnson said. *"They are smart. They value what they do. They respect it. They show up and they really try to get better."*

Those words reach far beyond athletics. They apply to boardrooms, classrooms, creative studios, and team meetings everywhere. This distinction, between talent and greatness, is something every leader and high performer must wrestle with.

Johnson posed a challenge that cuts to the heart of leadership and performance in any domain:

"You just can't rely on your talent. There are people out here that really study the game. I know you are talented, gifted, and skilled. But will you respect it enough? Like, respect it. When you respect something, you bring a certain spirit, perspective, and mentality to it."

In a world obsessed with shortcuts, where comfort is one tap away and cutting corners can still create the illusion of success, the real question for us is this: Will we still choose the path of mastery?

- Will we continue to study our craft?
- Will we stay curious about our industry?
- Will we honor our role by consistently elevating not just ourselves, but those we serve?

Every one of us has talent. Most organizations are filled with gifted individuals. But talent is only the entry point. The differentiator is mindset, character, and the daily pursuit of excellence, grounded in deep respect.

Respect for the craft. Respect for the process. Respect for the details.

It's the leader who studies their industry like a student. It's the coach who refines their approach after every season, even after success. It's the executive who builds vision not just on instinct, but on insight and a deep understanding of people.

As leaders, we aren't just managing performance, we're modeling it. We're showing our teams what excellence looks like when nobody's watching. We're setting a tone, a rhythm, a standard.

So the question isn't just: Are we talented?

It's: Do we respect the craft enough to keep learning? Do we study the game even after we've already won a few rounds? Do we bring a spirit to our work that elevates everyone around us?

When we model that, when we show up with intention, discipline, and a hunger to grow, we don't just improve. We raise the frequency of the culture around us.

So the next time you feel tempted to coast on talent alone, ask yourself: Do I respect this enough to study it? To outwork it? To get better, not just for me, but for the people I lead and serve?

Because that is the true difference, and the separator, between good and great.

JIMMY BUFFETT, THE STORYTELLER

Jimmy Buffett didn't sell music, books, food or boats. He sold escapism.

By using great stories, he took his audience to places they wanted to go but couldn't. Buffett was the shining example of living a carefree life without stress. Each of his songs, concerts or radio stations on Sirius moved his fans to his fictional place called Margaritaville, where the beer flowed, the sun shined, the drinks were cold, and there was the potential for finding a huge treasure.

"There was no such place as Margaritaville," Buffett once explained. "It was a made-up place in my mind, basically made up about my experiences in Key West and having to leave Key West and go on the road to work and then come back and spend time by the beach."

"It's pure escapism is all it is," he added. "I'm not the first one to do it, nor shall I probably be the last. But I think it's really a part of the human condition that you've got to have some fun. You've got to get away from whatever you do to make a living or other parts of life that stress you out. I try to make it at least 50/50 fun to work, and so far, it's worked out."

Buffett never received high praise from music critics for his songwriting or albums and never had a No. 1 record. Still, he had a loyal audience called Parrotheads, who supported his career.

He wasn't a great singer or guitarist, even admitting that others were far more talented. What made Buffett effective was his ability to tell powerful stories.

No leader can achieve anything without the power of being a great storyteller.

As storytelling expert Karen Eber writes in her book, *The Perfect Story,* our brains have "five factory settings" that impact how we engage with and interpret information.

When the storyteller understands how the brain operates and engages, the stories become an effective leadership tool.

1. **Lazy Brain.** According to Eber, the brain is lazy and wants to conserve calories to keep you alive. Great stories force the brain to spend calories by engaging the senses.
2. **Assumptions.** The brain continually makes predictions based on past experiences. Great stories slow down or harden these assumptions.
3. **Library of Files.** According to Eber, we process 34 gigabytes of information into our library of files. Great stories connect us to what we know through specific details and metaphors.
4. **In/Out Groups.** We feel part of a group when we hear a great story; there is a connection to others.
5. **Seek Pleasure and Avoid Pain.** The brain is wired to seek pleasure to avoid pain and discomfort. Storytelling makes us feel good, and as we listen to a good story, our brains light up.

What story are you telling? How much time do you spend shaping it to get those around you to feel their brains at work?

The more time we spend on storytelling, the more our leadership skills improve.

Buffett might not have been a great musician. But he understood the brain and told stories that allowed him to connect with millions all over the world.

He once said his "voyage was never a well-conceived plan; it was a made-up story as he went along."

At your next meeting, become Jimmy Buffett (without the flip flops) and tell a great story.

It will make a difference.

THE YEARS BEFORE THE BRIGHT LIGHTS

The gym was small. There was no seating on two of its sides, and maroon and yellow pads hugged the walls just feet from the court.

Behind the benches, a set of wooden bleachers stretched back about 10 rows, though very rarely were they ever filled.

For years, that tiny gym was home to Tobin Anderson, head men's basketball coach at St. Thomas Aquinas College in Sparkill, N.Y., just 20 miles north of Manhattan.

Fast forward to a Friday night in 2023, and Anderson was coaching in a slightly bigger venue, with a slightly bigger audience.

He led the No. 16-seed Fairleigh Dickinson Knights to one of the greatest upsets in college basketball history, knocking off No. 1 seed Purdue, 63-58, in front of nearly 20,000 fans in Columbus, Ohio.

And yet, it's the tiny gym that might be the most important part of the story.

Because just about all of us as leaders harbor some ambitious dream. We want to take over the company, run the school district, or bring our vision and philosophy to a team that needs a lift. Some of us get the chance. Others never do.

But Anderson's improbable, decades-long journey offers two critical lessons worth remembering:

1. There are immensely talented people at all levels.

We often assume the very best in any industry are found in the most prestigious positions. We reason that the top doctors work at elite hospitals, the greatest coaches with powerhouse franchises, the brightest minds at Ivy League institutions.

But FDU's win reminds us: there are gifted people everywhere. Talent doesn't always sit under the brightest spotlight. Sometimes, all it takes is the right opportunity for a person's skill set to become undeniable.

2. We never know when our chance may come

Anderson spent nearly 25 years coaching at the Division II and III levels, often in front of 100 or 200 spectators, before finally getting a Division I opportunity.

The truth is, many of us toil away in relative obscurity, hoping our consistency, character, and results will eventually attract the right eyes. It's easy to grow discouraged or cynical when progress feels slow or unnoticed.

But real leadership requires faith. Faith that if we keep doing the right things, keep executing with excellence, keep building authentic relationships, and keep staying true to our vision, our opportunity will come.

Anderson and his team will be remembered for decades for their historic win.

But the roots of that upset weren't planted in Columbus that week, or even in the practices leading up to the tournament.

They were planted years earlier, in the solitude of small gyms with empty bleachers, by a coach who wasn't chasing the next opportunity but pouring everything he had into the one right in front of him.

'WHAT COULD I BE MISSING HERE?'

Her photo was plastered on the covers of the most respected business magazines in the country.

"The Next Steve Jobs," *Inc.* declared.

"This CEO Is Out For Blood," *Fortune* stated.

"The Freshman," *Forbes* headlined, paired with a dramatic black-and-white portrait.

Yet not long after, Elizabeth Holmes, the former Theranos CEO once hailed as a transformative executive, was sentenced to 11 years in prison for defrauding investors over her blood-testing company's faulty technology and misleading business practices.

Why does this matter? Why should coaches, executives, and teachers care about the sentencing of someone many may never have even followed?

Because beyond the clear moral failures, the most relevant takeaway is this: what happens when we make rash assumptions and leap to conclusions without properly vetting a candidate.

As leaders, we often want to be ahead of the curve.

We spot a gifted prospect at a tournament and immediately extend a scholarship before others do. We make a recent college graduate a full-time offer after a few impressive weeks. We dismiss the intern's arrogance because of raw talent that could make a difference.

But when something, or someone, appears appealing, another critical question must be asked: What could I be missing here? What are the hidden risks?

Theranos had major problems from the start. Its machines, supposedly able to run 1,000 health tests from a single finger prick, didn't work. Holmes herself often struggled to explain the science.

Yet because she looked the part of a powerful CEO, commanded attention with her deep voice, and carried a veneer of charisma, the media, investors, and public overlooked the flaws in order to get ahead of the competition.

The lesson isn't to become cynical of every opportunity or to doubt everything we encounter.

It's this: leaders can do real damage to their organizations if they fail to rigorously vet character, skills, and credibility. Because sometimes, what looks too good to be true really is.

THE VALUE OF OUR WORD

As Mike Tomlin guided his teenage son through the college football recruitment process, he gave him a firm order: *"If you make a commitment to a university, your recruitment process is over. That's where we're going."*

Tomlin, the Pittsburgh Steelers head coach, wanted his son to understand that his word meant something, that pledges weren't to be thrown around loosely or reneged upon when something shinier came along.

These days, though, commitments often look less like etched-in-stone guarantees and more like vague agreements or temporary intentions.

Players select schools, then back out when a more enticing offer appears. Coaches sign multi-year contracts, only to bolt at the first opportunity. Executives promise results, deadlines, and sweeping changes, only to watch those targets pass unmet.

As leaders, we must recognize how easy it is to become prisoners of the moment, to say something that feels right when momentum is on our side.

But our players, employees, and team members are counting on us to be credible, to paint a realistic picture of what's ahead, not just say whatever will make us popular in the short term.

The constant shuffling, "pivoting," and chasing of better options doesn't just affect optics, it affects people's lives. We have a moral and ethical duty not to oversell and underdeliver.

As Tomlin put it: "Your word means something."

What are some elements to consider?

- **Gather the facts first.** Don't commit until you have the full picture.
- **Test the impulse.** Will you feel the same way in a week, or are you just reacting in the moment?
- **Build in a cooling-off period.** Give yourself 24 hours before making a critical decision.
- **Remember the ripple effect.** Your promises impact more than just you. They shape the lives and plans of others.

Of course, unforeseen circumstances, weather, injury, family tragedy, can force adjustments. That's reality.

But the larger point is this: when we promise the world to our players, students, or employees, we shouldn't lead them to another galaxy.

WHO WE LEAD

Rick Pitino had done just about everything over his illustrious basketball coaching career. He achieved success in the NBA, won college national championships, and turned around a team in Europe.

But Pitino was determined not to slow down. He took on the challenge of coaching at Iona College in suburban New York, far from the pomp and pageantry of the University of Kentucky, Louisville or the Boston Celtics.

He knew he wasn't coaching the best. He didn't have five-star recruits on his roster or play his home games at a 20,000-seat arena.

But Pitino was happy, not because he was back coaching the game he loved but because he got to do it the way he really wanted.

Pitino removed all of the trappings from himself and his Iona team, which once pulled off a remarkable upset over a highly ranked Alabama squad.

There were no more plush offices, corner suites or private jets. Instead, he spent his life teaching to an engaged audience. He had a team of players eager to learn, eager to embrace his knowledge, eager to improve their craft.

He didn't have to worry about playing time for the elite recruit or parents complaining that he was holding their sons back. He coached freely and taught the ones who wanted to be taught. For all of his glory and past success, Pitino made a real difference because his players were willing to let him.

Who we lead is as important as how we lead. When we compromise our beliefs to acquire bigger names, with the idea of winning more games or earning more money, then we lose the freedom of being ourselves. We might have more talent, but our strength as the leader rarely reaches its full potential. When we have to oversell our program to potential recruits, we compromise our ability to teach and influence. And when we take players who have high-level talent but don't fit our program or values, our success level often rapidly declines. Boosters may be happy the school landed a top recruit, but the ripple effect of the signing can cause massive headaches.

Instead of taking five-stars, Pitino took two- and three-stars and turned them into four-stars every day. Over time, he was able to compete at the highest level of college basketball again because his players constantly got better.

Developing the right culture was never easy. Pitino had an advantage at Iona because he didn't have the resources, so saying no to top recruits' demands was easy. His bluechip recruit was himself and his uncanny ability to make players better.

When we bring in the right people instead of the most talented ones, we'll see significant growth in our teams and become far happier as leaders.

In whatever industry we are in, when we know the type of personnel we want, we'll steadily get better. We may never win the recruiting titles, but we can win the title that matters most, on the field, in the boardroom, in the classroom.

Most of all, we'll really enjoy our jobs. Just ask Rick Pitino.

WHY WE SHOULD BE IN FOUNDER MODE

In a post on his website, programmer and investor Paul Graham wrote about hearing Brian Chesky, the founder of Airbnb, discuss the pitfalls companies face when they grow from start-ups into large enterprises.

When Chesky started Airbnb, he devoted every waking hour to his project. What began as a simple idea quickly grew into a huge business, with advice pouring in from all directions about "what's next."

As the company expanded, Chesky shifted from founder to manager. He listened to highly successful leaders who told him: hire smart, talented people and then step back.

But the result? Airbnb began to unravel.

As things slipped away, Chesky studied how Steve Jobs ran Apple and quickly decided to return to founder mode. Graham coined the term in his essay, and it has since become a buzzword in the corporate world.

Here's the breakdown of the two leadership styles:

Founder Mode

- Deep involvement in all aspects of the business
- Hands-on approach and attention to detail
- Direct engagement with employees at all levels
- Driven by vision and passion for the mission
- Often associated with intensity and micromanagement

Proponents argue founder mode allows for:

- Faster decision-making
- Preservation of the company's original vision and culture

- More innovative and disruptive approaches

Manager Mode

- Delegation of responsibilities to direct reports
- Focus on high-level strategy and oversight
- Reliance on management practices and structures
- Emphasis on processes and scalability

Advocates claim manager mode enables:

- Better scalability for growing companies
- More sustainable work-life balance
- Development of a strong leadership team

Consider David Chase. When he struggled to sell his television series idea, *The Sopranos*, HBO finally gave him a chance. For the next seven years, Chase remained in founder mode.

The Sopranos was his creation. Every word, every scene required his approval. Even when he didn't write the script, he outlined the season, stayed deeply involved in the final product, and devoted his life to the show. His actors and writers often bristled at the intensity, but they also knew his detail and devotion set the standard.

The same dynamic plays out in sports. A young assistant becomes a first-time head coach, and early on, lets assistants run their areas unchecked, partly because, as assistants themselves, they never wanted interference from the head coach. But only when that new coach steps fully into founder mode does the team adopt an identity and reflect the leader's personality.

HIRING

For leaders in any field, achieving success, whether in a start-up or in a bigger role, isn't a reason to step back. It's an incentive to step forward and become even more involved, protecting both the vision and the product.

All great companies, teams, and organizations are built on the foundation of founder mode. Once they shift fully to manager mode, the decline begins.

Being a founder is hard. Staying successful is even harder. But one truth remains: letting others take control of your dream won't ever work. Embrace the hard. Stay in founder mode.

EVALUATE

STORIES ON EVALUATING

UNDERSTANDING THE PEOPLE WE LEAD

"How can what seems to be many really be one? How can what is one manifest as many? Just what is it that there are many of, and what is it that remains one throughout?"

The Fisherman's Tomb: The True Story of the Vatican's Secret Search
– John O'Neill

One of the more famous photographs taken during the 18th century captured a Comanche woman tightly clutching her daughter. The photo was prominently featured in several American history books for students to learn about the dangerous Wild West.

The only problem was that the woman was not a Comanche. She was Cynthia Ann Parker, a young lady of a privileged white family. Parker was captured at the age of 10 during a Comanche raid on her family's compound and lost many of her relatives in the violent clash. For the next 24 years, she would live as a Comanche woman. She married a Comanche chief, had two sons and one daughter and integrated herself into the Comanche way of life. Her birth blood was Caucasian. But her lifeblood was Comanche.

In 1860, during the famous battle of The Pease River, Parker's husband, Peta Nocona, died defending her. Parker would return to life in Texas, but once back home, she frequently attempted to run away, clinging to the Comanche culture she had grown to embrace.

Her family members thought Parker was mentally ill. No one could understand how or why she would ever want to return to that horrible way of life. But no one from Cynthia Ann Parker's biological family really put forth the effort to understand her.

Everyone expected her to be happy because their way of life had to be the best. No one saw life from Cynthia's point of view. This unique problem happens to all leaders and coaches. When we fail to appreciate the backgrounds of the people we lead and do not spend time studying their lives, we fail as leaders. We assume our followers are willing to walk in our direction because of our title and compensation package. That assumption fails us almost every time.

Leadership is about uniting people. Yet, how can we unite without understanding everyone's background? Without a powerful connection gained through acknowledgment, we cannot motivate, develop trust, and, most of all, demand excellence. We become the boss, not the leader; the enforcer, not the influencer.

When recruiting talent for our team in any profession, we must be diligent in learning about different cultures within our base. If we want to have a diversified and inclusive group, the leader must have a complete understanding of the cultural imprints of those who join the organization.

Learn about the people you lead. Learn not only the names of their family members. But also learn their thought process and their heritage. It will allow you to understand how to get them to perform at their best.

Cynthia Ann Parker died misunderstood. She died away from her real Comanche family. And perhaps most tragic of all, she died with her maternal family never having appreciated the woman she had become.

THE 7 ELEMENTS OF TEAM COMPOSITION

It's a common philosophy across just about any industry: recruit the best and the brightest and plug them into your organization.

But sometimes what prospects have in talent, they lack in other areas. We're confident we can mold them and that they'll shape up once they're in our system. But too often, the pieces just don't fit.

Whether we're recruiting players for a college basketball program, building a sales team, or hiring new personnel at a hospital, there are seven pivotal factors, along with a host of questions, that we should consider:

Talent: How skilled is this person we're considering bringing on?

Character: What are this person's values and morals?

Fit: How well will they mesh with other team members?

Fix: What existing weakness of ours does this person address?

Value: How will he/she make our organization better?

Risk: What are the red flags? What could go wrong?

Trust: Will this person be reliable and dependable at all times?

Across these seven categories, let's rank our prospects 1–4:

4 = extraordinary

3 = good

2 = average

1 = poor

An organization doesn't necessarily have to give equal consideration to each factor.

What's important is finding a weighted scale of these seven that fits your leadership philosophy.

Often, the most important element of team composition isn't deciding whom to add. It's choosing whom to rule out.

THE TRUTH TEST: WHAT "GOOD WILL HUNTING" TEACHES US ABOUT AUTHENTIC HIRING

In the film *Good Will Hunting*, the character Will Hunting, portrayed by Matt Damon, demonstrates his extraordinary memory and authenticity during a pivotal scene with Skylar, his girlfriend, played by Minnie Driver. This moment reveals not only the brilliance of Will's mind but also the depth and complexity of his character.

Will, a janitor at MIT with exceptional mathematical abilities, carries a tumultuous past filled with trauma and personal struggle. Despite his genius, his life is riddled with challenges that block his potential. The story begins to unfold when Professor Gerald Lambeau discovers Will's anonymous solution to a complex math problem and attempts to steer him toward a brighter future. But Will's violent tendencies and legal troubles prompt Lambeau to enlist the help of therapist Sean Maguire, brought to life by the late Robin Williams.

Through their sessions, Sean helps Will confront his pain, peel back his emotional armor, and begin to recognize his worth beyond intellect.

One scene in particular stands out.

During a conversation with Skylar, Will casually mentions that he has twelve big brothers. Taken aback, she challenges him to name them all. Without hesitation, Will rattles off all twelve names. Still skeptical, Skylar demands he do it again immediately. Once more, Will delivers flawlessly.

What seems like a charming exchange between two characters actually reveals something deeper: a powerful technique for assessing authenticity.

Skylar's method, asking for immediate repetition, functions like a real-time integrity check. It gauges not just memory, but truthfulness. And it holds practical value beyond the screen, particularly in high-stakes environments like hiring and leadership evaluation. In any workplace, authenticity is more than a buzzword. It's a competitive advantage. Hiring authentic individuals, those who are not only qualified but aligned with a team's values, can build trust, elevate culture, and boost long-term performance.

But how do we spot authenticity in an interview? Here are three practical techniques:

1. Behavioral Interviews

Behavioral interviews prompt candidates to share real-life examples of how they've navigated past situations. These questions help uncover core values like honesty, resilience, and teamwork. Examples: "Tell me about a time you faced an ethical dilemma at work. How did you handle it?" "Describe a moment when you had to give honest feedback to a colleague. What was the outcome?" These aren't just prompts—they're truth-seeking tools.

2. The Immediate Repetition Technique

Inspired by *Good Will Hunting*, this approach involves asking a candidate to repeat or restate key information from earlier in the interview. For example, if someone says they led a major initiative, ask them to summarize the same project details again later. Consistency often reveals character. The ability to retell without major variation suggests credibility and genuine experience.

3. Values Alignment Checks

Does the candidate live out your organization's values? Use situational judgment tests or real-life scenarios that reflect your team's culture. Ask: "Here's a core value we live by, can you share how you've embodied this in a past role?" "What part of our mission statement most resonates with you, and why?" These questions push past surface-level responses and move into alignment and fit.

We've all been fooled before. We've all wanted to believe someone was who they claimed to be, only to find out later that they weren't.

But by leaning into tools like behavioral interviewing, values alignment, and yes, even repetition, we can better navigate the tough terrain of hiring and surround ourselves with people who are not only smart and skilled, but real.

Because in leadership, in sports, in business, and in life, authenticity always endures.

WHY EVERY LEADER NEEDS A SWOT ANALYSIS

John Roselli was unlike any other organized crime figure. Handsome and charismatic, earning him the nickname "Handsome Johnny," he operated at the unique crossroads of organized crime, Hollywood glamour, and covert government operations. Roselli wasn't just a mafia man; he was deeply involved in the movie industry, collaborated with the CIA on clandestine projects, and managed to avoid the early demise that so often befell those in his world.

When Roselli handed out his business card, it bore his name boldly alongside the single word: "Strategist."

Without the benefit of formal education or a business school degree, Roselli instinctively applied principles akin to SWOT analysis (Strengths, Weaknesses, Opportunities, and Threats) to navigate his perilous environment. His ability to assess situations, provide sound advice to his partners, and deliver consistent results proved invaluable. This skill set not only kept him alive but also ensured prosperity for those he worked with.

For Roselli, this analysis was a matter of life or death. As leaders, while our stakes may not be as dramatic, we face our own dual challenges: the need to develop a personal strategy to improve ourselves and a professional strategy to showcase our value. The two are inextricably linked. Without the former, the latter falters.

Roselli exemplified a deep understanding of his own strengths and limitations. By leveraging his talents, he walked a tightrope through one of the most dangerous fields imaginable.

There's much we can learn from his approach:

Strengths
These are internal attributes and resources that drive success. Assessing what you or your organization does well is crucial. Make it a habit to list your strengths monthly and measure progress. Remember, strengths only remain impactful if they continue to shine.

Weaknesses
What areas need improvement? How are you addressing them? Improvement must be intentional and measurable. Like Roselli, avoid ventures that don't align with your core strengths.

Opportunities
These are external factors that allow you to showcase your talents and add value. This isn't about self-promotion; it's about leveraging your abilities to serve your team and organization effectively.

Threats
External challenges can jeopardize success. Anticipating obstacles and crafting strategies to mitigate them is vital for sustained achievement. Nothing ever goes exactly as planned, so understanding and preparing for potential threats is key.

Leaders, and those aspiring to lead, should conduct a comprehensive SWOT analysis on a monthly basis. This practice helps us evaluate where we stand, where we're headed, and how to improve.

Like Roselli, honing your ability to strategize gives you a critical advantage. Only by truly knowing your SWOT can you provide valuable insights, make informed decisions, and earn the title of "Strategist."

THE FOUR P'S

Branch Rickey, the former Brooklyn Dodgers General Manager, was instrumental in breaking the color barrier in Major League Baseball when he signed Jackie Robinson. Rickey pioneered creating the farm system, which allowed teams to develop talent at varying levels of play. While a member of the St. Louis Cardinals organization, he established a minor league team in Fostoria, Ohio, and encouraged local talent to try out for a spot with the Fostoria Firebirds.

One of the young players attempting to make the team was Anthony Lucadello, who grew up in Chicago, Illinois. Lucadello was a marginal prospect, playing just two seasons and working at the Fostoria Screw Company to pay his bills. But Tony yearned for baseball. He required the ballpark and the competition to make him feel complete. Lucadello knew his career as a player was going to be brief; therefore, he needed an alternative plan.

Tony Lucadello devised a plan to hold tryouts for other prospects in the Fostoria area, to assemble a team of players who would compete against other minor league clubs around the Midwest. One of his players, pitcher Bob Rush, got invited to try out for the Chicago Cubs. After the tryout, Cubs owner Philip Wrigley said, before we sign Rush, we better hire this young man right here. Wrigley said, "This young man, pointing to Tony Lucadello, was born to scout."

Philip Wrigley proved to be a prophet and utterly right about Tony. Lucadello had a tremendous MLB career as a scout, discovering seven All-Stars and two Hall of Famers, in Philadelphia Phillies third baseman Mike Schmidt and Chicago Cubs pitcher Ferguson Jenkins.

Tony Lucadello broke down all scouts in four different areas, which all started with the letter P:

Poor Scout: A scout that cannot see talent.

Picker Scout: A scout that "picks" on one thing a player cannot do well.

Production Scout: A scout that only uses production to justify their evaluation.

Projector Scout: A scout that can project the player into the future.

Now, we all want to become the best Projector Scout when evaluating talent. We want to be able to recognize talent with the ability to utilize that talent in the right manner. Talent, along with skill development in the correct role, is a successful formula.

In each part of our daily life, we are continually evaluating talent and opportunities. Make mental notes of the four P's when discussing talent evaluation. Hold yourself and others accountable to think about projecting the talent, not merely labeling the talent.

We can also use the Lucadello method for "evaluating the evaluator," to make sure we are not falling into a destructive trap of listening to the wrong people. Most people are good at evaluating the obvious. The exceptional leaders will look beneath the surface and see what others don't see, while possessing the wisdom and courage to see beyond the obvious.

Tony Lucadello loved his work deeply. He took great pride in his ability to evaluate talent correctly. When the Philadelphia Phillies forced him to retire in the spring of 1989, at the age of seventy-six, he could not live without having baseball in his life. Tragically, he committed suicide on a baseball field in Fostoria.

To best remember Tony, let's find ways to utilize his Four P's every day. It would make him proud.

THE UNDERCOOKED STEAK

The visit has gone perfectly. The top recruit gets along with potential teammates, is impressed by the program's facilities, and gives thoughtful answers to the coach's routine questions.

But then, at dinner with the coaching staff, the steak comes back undercooked. Annoyed, the player snaps at the server and complains that it's maybe the worst meal he's ever had.

That single moment offers a glimpse into what long-time University of Oklahoma Women's Basketball Coach Sherri Coale called a crucial, yet often undervalued, element of evaluation: watching how prospects "do life."

"People can come up with the right answers to boxed questions and tell you all the things you want to hear, and you can look at a résumé and see all the things you want to see," she said on The Learning Leader Show with Ryan Hawk. *"But the best decisions are the ones that are void of all the strings pulling at you."*

Coale explained that she considered questions beyond highlight tapes and recruiting rankings when evaluating top prospects:

How do they respond when their food comes back cold?

How do they handle a flight delay?

How do they interact in a room full of people who can't do anything for them?

"We can want a thing to work so badly because of what the paper says," she noted.

The lesson isn't to trick candidates with adversity tests or to overemphasize minor character flaws. It's to recognize that résumés, highlight reels, and interview answers only tell part of the story. Real insight comes from observing how people navigate the ordinary friction of life.

Because before we celebrate our brilliant new hire or top recruit, we should ask ourselves: Have we truly watched how they "do life"?

After all, once we offer them that top cut of steak, there's really no sending it back.

'THE NUMBERS STINK'

The Purdue Boilermakers finished the men's college basketball regular season ranked among the top 10 in the country during the 2021-2022 season despite not having a single five-star high school recruit on their roster.

So how does this happen? How does a team with seemingly ordinary talent for its level punch so far above its weight?

Some of this success can certainly be attributed to coaching and skill development, but, according to Coach Matt Painter, it's also because there are various intangibles that rankings can't measure. "I hate the numbers. The numbers stink," Painter once said about recruiting. "When you rank guys, you can't measure what's in their heart. When you go and recruit them and spend time with them and see them, you see that."

It's a crucial message for us as leaders.

So often, we try to put projections, labels and stereotypes on our team members. We typecast them into various roles based on our expectations and our own past experiences.

Too small. Didn't graduate from a prestigious-enough university. Has an odd accent. Didn't perform well on this project. Is different than what we're accustomed to.

While these assessments are merited at times, they often hinder our ability to cultivate our teams and develop our personnel.

Painter seems to have figured this out, tossing expectations and the opinions of outsiders aside while honing in on the relevant intangibles for his program.

"The evaluation is your work ethic," he said. "Do you have any baggage?"

As we as leaders proceed with our scouting, our talent recruitment and our employee evaluations, we might be wise to reflect on Painter's words and dig a little deeper to find the non-obvious.

The hidden gems can often end up sparkling the brightest.

THE RULE OF THIRDS: OLYMPIAN ALEXI PAPPAS ON CHASING DREAMS & EMBRACING CRAPPY DAYS

Alexi Pappas is an Olympic athlete, award-winning writer, poet, filmmaker, author of *Bravey: Chasing Dreams, Befriending Pain, and Other Big Ideas,* and so much more.

A record-setting runner, Alexi set the Greek national record in the 10,000 meters and competed for Greece at the 2016 Olympic Games. Equally gifted as a storyteller, her words have graced the pages of *The New York Times, Runner's World, Women's Running Magazine, Sports Illustrated, The Atlantic,* and *Outside.*

In a thought-provoking conversation on the *Rich Roll Podcast,* Alexi shared a powerful framework that reshaped how she approaches both competition and creativity: The Rule of Thirds.

This life-changing perspective, instilled in her by her Olympic coach after a grueling workout at Hayward Field in Eugene, Oregon, has transformed how she pursues big dreams across multiple passions.

"So my Olympic coach told me after a particularly challenging workout where I could not hit my splits before going to the Rio Olympics, that that was OK. It was the Rule of Thirds. And he was an Olympian, you know, I always soaked in everything he said.

And I was like, what's the Rule of Thirds? And he said, when you're chasing a dream or doing anything hard, you're meant to feel good a third of the time, OK a third of the time, and crappy a third of the time. And if the ratio is roughly in that range, then you're doing fine. So today was the crappy day along your dream chasing. Right? And if the ratio is off, like you feel too good all the time or too bad, then you've got to look at whether you're fatiguing or not trying hard enough or pushing yourself."

Her coach's words contain a simple yet profound truth: struggle isn't a sign of failure, it's a natural and expected part of meaningful progress. When we embrace this mindset, we stop resisting discomfort and start seeing it as a necessary checkpoint on the road to excellence and transformation.

We won't always feel our best. That's life and leadership. That's what makes the journey intriguing. But how we respond on those "crappy" and "OK" days is fully within our control.

What if, instead of resisting those tough moments, we leaned into them? What if we used them as unique opportunities to sharpen our skills, assess what's working (or not), and refine our approach? Showing up and giving our best even on the hardest and crappiest days is what separates those who merely dream from those who step into the arena to compete and achieve.

As leaders and high performers, we should also extend this mindset to our teams. A bad day doesn't necessarily mean we're off course, sometimes it just means we're pushing boundaries. Instead of overcorrecting too quickly or reacting purely out of emotion, we should pause, lean in, and assess what is actually transpiring, encouraging reflection, presence, and effort. Neither of which requires elite talent.

Too often, the mind becomes the biggest obstacle, convincing us to quit when things feel tough. But setbacks are not signals to stop; they are proof that we are engaged in something that matters. Don't let the mind bully the body into quitting on the crappy days.

If the goals and dreams we are chasing truly mean something, we will keep showing up regardless of how we feel in the moment. If they don't, we will likely find an excuse. Are we truly committed to the things we say we want, even long after the mood we set them in has passed?

You will likely experience one of these three types of days today: good, OK, or crappy.

No matter where you land, ask yourself: Will I still show up? Will I lean in and give my best to the moment? Will I trust the process and keep stacking the days?

Momentum is built through these daily choices. Each small effort and action, especially on the difficult days, compounds into something greater and far more meaningful. That's how personal and professional breakthroughs happen.

Keep trusting yourself. You are more than enough. Keep showing up for yourself and those you lead, while keeping your why and the Rule of Thirds top of mind.

THE 6 TYPES OF GENIUS

Leaders come in all shapes, sizes, and styles, and no two are the same.

Just ask Pat Lencioni, author of *The Six Dysfunctions of a Team* and a dozen other best-selling leadership and management books.

Lencioni begins each book with a fable, setting the stage for a lesson on improvement. In his book *Working Genius*, he breaks down various styles of leaders, categorizing different natural talents and strengths that individuals possess in the workplace.

His six include:

Wonder
This genius involves seeing the potential and asking questions that challenge the status quo. People with this genius are often curious and imaginative, excelling at envisioning new possibilities and exploring uncharted territory.

Invention
This genius is characterized by generating new and innovative ideas. Individuals with this genius have a knack for creating solutions, thinking outside the box, and developing novel approaches to problems.

Discernment
This genius is about evaluating ideas and options with a critical eye. People with this genius have strong judgment and can effectively analyze information, identify risks and pitfalls, and make sound decisions through careful evaluation.

Galvanizing
This genius involves rallying and inspiring others toward a common purpose. Those with this genius can motivate

and energize teams, create unity, and ignite enthusiasm and commitment to a shared goal.

Enablement
This genius supports and enables others to achieve their best work. Individuals with this genius excel at developing people's potential, providing resources and guidance, and fostering a supportive and empowering environment.

Tenacity
This genius represents perseverance in overcoming obstacles and challenges. People with this genius have a strong work ethic, determination, and the capacity to stay focused and committed to achieving goals, even in the face of adversity.

For any leader, it's hugely beneficial to understand how you fit into these categories. Identifying with one offers an opportunity to improve if we're honest and willing to self-evaluate. If we're someone who is being led, these categories help us better understand the process.

Once we process the "how" and the "why," we can accelerate our personal growth and development.

What makes Lencioni's list even more impactful is that some leaders possess more than one trait, allowing them to shine in different lights while elevating their teams over the long term.

THE 4 STEPS OF RISK EVALUATION

Vinod Khosla, an Indian-American entrepreneur and co-founder of Sun Microsystems, built his reputation as a visionary investor known for both groundbreaking successes and instructive failures that shaped his enduring approach to innovation and leadership.

Khosla authored *Gene Pool Engineering for Entrepreneurs,* where he notably wrote: "The goal of gene pool engineering is first to create a culture where multiple people engage in problem-solving, and team members share best practices from previous organizations and a diverse set of backgrounds for the specific problems being addressed."

Khosla's gene pool approach has a four-step plan for entrepreneurs when hiring talent to help them launch their start-up off the ground and run seamlessly. Although intended for entrepreneurs, Khosla's advice is vital to anyone who accepts a new position or is looking for ways to solve current problems.

1. **Identify the five largest risks involved in the decision.**

    Examine everything by asking why something won't be successful instead of assuming everything will go as planned. From the risk list, you then start to look for employees. Without understanding your risks, you could never build a successful company.

2. **Define the skill set necessary to address those risks.**

    Hire people who fit that skill set, not ones who are friends or past workmates. Make sure whomever you hire has expertise in the risk areas.

3. **Hire the best problem solver, not the person who worked for the problem solver.**

   This occurs in sports often when owners or athletic directors hire coaches from successful programs and then wonder why their new coach does not have the same talent to make decisions. Don't hire people who are associated with greatness; hire those who have great potential.

4. **Diversity in Thought.**

   Hire two or three people who have diverse backgrounds and are qualified to address each of the risks. In the end, you should have a diverse team.

The key lesson from Khosla that we can all benefit from lies in understanding and correctly identifying risk. If we miss on risk evaluation, then the entire operation can fall apart.

As we sit in our office, classroom, or boardroom today, let's write down the five biggest risks to our future, and then set out to follow the Khosla plan.

CRICHTON, GELL-MANN AMNESIA AND THE NFL DRAFT

What do Michael Crichton, NFL Draft grades, and Murray Gell-Mann all have in common?

Crichton was an American author and television writer who penned over 26 novels, selling more than 200 million copies worldwide. After graduating from medical school, Crichton bypassed becoming a doctor and instead used his knowledge to write science-fiction thrillers such as *Jurassic Park* and *Twister*.

He is also credited with developing the Gell-Mann Amnesia Effect, named after an American physicist who won a Nobel Peace Prize for his theory of elementary particles.

After every NFL Draft, teams are graded on their selections by members of the media who have evaluated the prospects. Draft grades then typically make a fan base happy, irate, or extremely sad.

The three tie together in this manner. When an NFL executive is reading a poor draft grade for his team, he can then cast doubt on the credentials of the evaluator. He finds multiple errors in the report and becomes exasperated and upset, giving the author no credibility.

But when the same executive reads another team's grade, good or bad, done by the same author, he believes every word, as if the evaluator somehow improved.

"I refer to it by this name because I once discussed it with Murray Gell-Mann, and by dropping a famous name, I imply greater importance to myself, and to the effect, than it would otherwise have," Crichton said.

We all fall victim to the Gell-Mann Amnesia Effect at times. When we read something we have deep knowledge and understanding of, we become critical and skeptical of the validity of the information. When we transfer to another subject outside our expertise, we believe everything written, never questioning the information.

As leaders, what we have to understand is that there are few true experts and even fewer with insight into our specific decision-making process. If we let an unqualified opinion create added uncertainty, then subconsciously, we will hinder our process the next time.

Making high or low-level decisions always comes with second-guessing. But if we pick and choose whose opinions we value, despite limited expertise behind them, then we can easily begin making decisions aimed at pleasing the assessor instead of doing what we know is right.

Ask any executive if he would rather have an A today and a bad team two years from now, or a D and a good team?

We know the answer. So instead of falling victim to amnesia, we need to ignore the noise and do what we believe is in our best interest.

Trust your area of expertise, and few others.

CHANGING MINDS: THREE KINDS OF TRUTH

"The mind is meant to know the truth. Train your mind to speak the truth in a committed language so it is beautiful and effective."
— **Yogi Bhajan**

One morning late in his life, renowned comedian Bob Hope was having breakfast at his home in Palm Springs, California. As the news played in the background, Hope heard a special report alert come on. The television reporter announced with great sadness the passing of legendary comic Bob Hope at the tender age of ninety-five. Hope continued his meal with a chuckle. But the reporting did not stop. Before an hour had passed, the Speaker of the United States House of Representatives, Dick Armey, ordered Representative Bob Stump to announce to Congress the news of Bob Hope's passing. With glowing accolades, praise, and condolences, the nation learned of the passing of this legend.

Bob Hope never flinched. Not because he was too old or incoherent, but because he knew the absolute truth. Hope was not going to overreact to something he heard or read when it was not fact. No matter how many sources confirmed his death, Bob Hope knew he was still breathing, still moving, and most importantly, still living.

It took almost eight hours for the Associated Press to retract the story. Representative Armey had to go before Congress apologizing for his mistake. Since Bob Hope was a comedian, this false story turned into a joke. While we can all play it off as a joke, in reality, we have all reacted to fake news and misinformation. We have believed reports even when we knew the absolute truth.

There are three different types of truth we all deal with each day:

Correspondence Theory of Truth

This theory states that a statement (a proposition) is true if it corresponds to or reflects reality. If somebody says, "It is raining" (the proposition), then it is true only if it is raining outside (reality).

Coherence Theory of Truth

This theory states that a statement (a proposition) is true if it is consistent with other things that are considered true (and do not contradict it). A proposition is true if it "fits into the system." For example, you hear a pencil falling to the ground. A second person in the room also hears it, and the pencil that you just saw on your table a moment ago is now gone. Three observations fit together: you hear it, a second person hears it, and the pencil is missing. According to the coherence theory, the proposition "the pencil hit the ground" is correct.

Pragmatic Theory of Truth

This theory states that something is true if it is useful. Whether or not it reflects reality is of minor importance. Somebody may, for example, believe that earning a lot of money is an essential thing in one's life. This belief is true for this person, and it is indeed a beneficial belief.

Next time you hear a report or believe something to be accurate, make sure you qualify the information into one of these truth theories. Had U.S. Representative Dick Armey done this, Bob Hope's breakfast would have been more enjoyable that day.

'ARE YOU ABOUT WINNING?'

Jerome Tang's Kansas State Wildcats were knocked out of the NCAA Men's Basketball Tournament during the 2022-23 season, but the coach provided some critical lessons to all leaders throughout a memorable season in Manhattan.

In one message in particular, Tang insisted he did not want to hear his players talk about winning, instead urging them to display their commitment through their actions. It's an essential reminder for us as leaders, and what makes the video all the more impactful is that Tang also issues a warning to himself, conveying that the commitment and discipline that go into achievement run two ways.

Success didn't just depend on the Wildcat players that year. Tang made it abundantly clear that it also fell on himself.

Los Angeles Lakers legend Kobe Bryant is a tremendous role model for any young athlete. Countless aspiring athletes have reminders of Bryant hanging in their room or on the sneakers they wear.

But do their actions match Kobe's?

When interviewing a potential candidate for a position on your team, ask them who they admire, then ask what three things they do similar to that person.

Next, make them tell you in specific detail what and when they adhere to these principles. If the candidates boast they have the Mamba Mentality, for example, ask what Kobe's 10 rules are and make them explain how those habits are incorporated into their life.

1. Get better every single day
2. Prove them wrong

3. Work on your weaknesses
4. Execute what you practiced
5. Learn from greatness
6. Learn from wins and losses
7. Practice mindfulness
8. Be ambitious
9. Believe in your team
10. Learn storytelling

If they don't know these 10 rules or can't give examples of their actions, kindly ask them to take Kobe's picture down out of respect to him.

Then, remind them what Tang says in the video: "You are committed toward winning."

SELECT

STORIES ON SELECTING

THE 3 TYPES OF UNDERACHIEVERS

The 1993 movie *A Bronx Tale* tells the story of a teenage boy, Calogero, facing the temptations of an easy but crime-infested mafia life versus staying on the blue-collar path of his bus-driving father, Lorenzo.

"The saddest thing in life is wasted talent," Lorenzo tells his son.

Why would anyone waste their talent? Why would someone with a God-given skillset not strive for greatness and stay on the hard-working path? And yet, we see it all the time.

Underachievers are the biggest tease on teams and in the workforce. They show flashes of dominance, but rarely display their skills consistently. Their inconsistency is maddening. They disappear, look lackluster, and leave their coach or leader wanting more.

We often wonder: How can I change this behavior? How can I make them more consistent? They bring enormous stress, and we grow frustrated when countless opportunities don't change the outcome.

But not all underachievers are alike. Too often, we lump them into one category and fail to see why some adapt while others never realize their potential. Is their inconsistency rooted in their own lack of drive, or in our inability to bring out the best in them?

There are three types of underachievers. Unless we evaluate each correctly, we risk wasting time and money trying to change the unchangeable.

Type 1: A.W.N.C.: All Work, No Compete

This type works hard, but when the moment matters most, they lack the competitive fire. If the path is easy, they shine. But in the biggest moments, they vanish. Leaders often fall in love with their work ethic, confusing it with competitiveness, and end up disappointed.

Type 2: N.W.N.C.: No Work, No Compete

This type has rare talent but no interest in being great. They act as if cursed with their gift. Their past is filled with one or two flashes of brilliance surrounded by long stretches of indifference.

Type 3: N.W.C.H.: No Work, Competes Hard

This type lacks consistent work habits and preparation, which ensures they underachieve. But when the lights come on, they compete with pride. Their effort gives them a chance, and if guided, their habits can improve.

Here's the truth: the only underachiever who can change is Type 3.

If someone has pride and a competitive spirit, you can teach them to build better work habits. But Types 1 and 2? They drain time, energy, and resources, and must be removed.

Talent without competitiveness is meaningless.

And that, as Lorenzo warned, is the true definition of wasted talent.

SOLDIER VS. SCOUT'S MINDSET

By the middle of the 1980s, Intel was struggling.

The once-powerful Silicon Valley giant had declined from an 82.9% market share in 1974 to a paltry 1.3% a decade later. Andy Grove, along with founders Robert Noyce and Gordon Moore, knew they had a big problem, and Intel's board of directors was growing increasingly nervous.

"The fact is that we had become a non-factor in DRAMs, with 2-3% market share," Grove said. "The DRAM business just passed us by! Yet, many people were still holding to the 'self-evident truth' that Intel was a memory company. One of the toughest challenges is to make people see that these self-evident truths are no longer true."

So Grove posed a question to Noyce and Moore in a meeting: "What would a new CEO do if we were ousted?"

Immediately, all three men knew they needed to shift the company's overall direction.

The question Grove asked is called the "Outsider Test." What would someone see from the outside that those living on the inside choose to ignore?

In her book *The Scout Mindset*, Julia Galef discusses the "Outsider Test" and how we can improve our judgment when we view problems from a scout's standpoint, instead of with a soldier's mindset. What's the difference?

A soldier seeks to defend his position, whereas a scout surveys and reports what is seen. Those are two vastly different viewpoints, and by posing the question peeking from the outside, Grove shifted Intel from a soldier's mindset to a scout's.

Galef believes that one of the biggest downfalls in shifting from soldier to scout is a bias called motivated reasoning, in which people filter out any information that goes against what they believe. When faced with a particular conclusion, people might then work backward and find ways to support that conclusion while ignoring evidence that supports alternatives. This cognitive bias can also manifest as changing one's opinion to match what one expects a social group would believe.

As leaders, we need to always ask ourselves when faced with decisions: Are we a scout or a soldier? Then ask: What would the new person do?

These two questions are the first steps to making better, non-biased choices.

THE NFL DRAFT AND SHOSHIN

The NFL Draft is one of the most highly anticipated events in sports, with teams investing millions of dollars to identify and select players who can transform their organizations.

But year after year, many still fall short.

As with any major decision, bias often plays a significant role in poor choices. Overconfidence in past experiences can also cloud judgment. The success rate of drafting talent remains roughly the same as it was decades ago, when teams relied on magazine rankings and word of mouth to make their picks.

Why hasn't talent forecasting improved despite all the advances in data and technology?

Economists Richard Thaler and Cade Massey once studied the history of the draft, analyzing where players were chosen and how they performed over time. Their findings were sobering.

Despite the vast time and money invested in scouting and analysis, teams were not very effective at predicting who would become great. Thaler and Massey concluded that there is only about a 52 percent chance that a player picked first will outperform a player taken later at the same position. In essence, NFL teams would be just as successful flipping a coin.

One possible reason for this lack of progress lies in a Zen Buddhism concept called *Shoshin*.

Shoshin means "beginner's mind," the belief that: "In the beginner's mind, there are many possibilities. In the expert's mind, there are few."

Many teams approach the draft as experts. They cling to familiar processes, avoid questioning their assumptions, and rarely express a willingness to be wrong. Conventional wisdom rules the day, even when it has proven ineffective.

In doing so, they fail to embody a beginner's mind, a mindset that welcomes curiosity, openness, and the freedom to explore.

They fail to be curious about new ways to evaluate talent. They rely on groupthink instead of independent thinking, judging success in the short term rather than the long term.

They resist embracing naivete, which Henry Ford once called "an infinite capacity to not know what can't be done."

Teams have worked tirelessly to improve their decision-making, but perhaps true progress will come not from more data, but from a renewed willingness to question how that data is used.

Maybe the next great breakthrough in drafting talent will come not from what teams know, but from what they are willing to unlearn.

ALL THE COACH WANTS

Skill. Talent. Athleticism.

They're often the elements that outsiders notice and the factors that draw attention to our teams.

But as coaches, we know better. We know what we value, what frequently determines success or disappointment, what allows us to get at least a little bit of sleep at night.

"Those guys who don't make mistakes, who know exactly who they are," former NBA coach and ESPN commentator Jeff Van Gundy said on *The Ryen Russillo Show.*

"I think mental strength is so important to being able to deal with the ups and downs, the peaks and valleys. Some of our star players are a little bit more up and down in those areas. To surround those guys with mentally strong guys is absolutely critical to get the success you want."

Ultimately, intense adversity is inevitable when we try to do anything at a high level, and talent alone isn't sufficient to defeat the daunting opponent or accomplish our ambitious goals.

It requires an uncommon resilience from our teams: that no matter what we've been through, we can stare the next challenge in the eyes and not blink. And while we may not always defeat it, we'll at least go down giving it everything we have.

Not all of our team members will have innate toughness, though. In fact, many won't.

It's on us as coaches and leaders to cultivate it and put our team members through as much realistic hardship in practices and rehearsals as we can, constantly reinforcing how important this resolve will be on the journey.

We as leaders would be wise to remind ourselves that sometimes, we might be better off turning to a tougher or more cerebral team member over a more talented one.

"Every time I put a dummy in and he'd do something dumb or we'd do something dumb, I wouldn't be mad at the guy, I'd be mad at myself," Van Gundy said.

"But tough, smart players. How often do they underachieve?"

BARRELS VS. AMMUNITION

What is the true test of knowing when to offer someone a promotion? How do we define what good job performance consists of? Is it long hours, how a person interacts with others, or how he/she plays the political game?

Keith Rabois, an early PayPal employee and venture capitalist, has some hard and fast rules to follow, detailing in a recent lecture how we can segment employees into two categories: "Barrels" and "Ammunition."

"Most great people actually are ammunition," he said. "But what you need in your company [startups in particular] are barrels."

How do we define and categorize each?

Barrels

- Can take an idea from its conception and transform it all the way to existing in the world, leading people to make it happen
- You give this person a project, goal, or problem, and that's the last instruction he/she needs

Ammunition

- Will do what they're told to the best of their ability
- Can be masters of a specialization

So, how do we evaluate whether someone is a barrel or ammunition?

Rabois suggests giving someone a difficult project, but small in scope, then seeing how they solve the entire problem.

"The other signal to look for is once you've hired someone with an open office, watch who goes up to other people's desks, particularly people they don't report to," he said. "If someone keeps going to some individual employee's desk and they don't report to them, it's a sign that they believe that person can help them. So, if you see that consistently, those are your barrels."

Finally, he suggests that any time you have an opportunity to take on a barrel, you should pull the trigger, even if you aren't hiring at that particular moment.

Want to improve your career or earn a promotion? Learn how to become a barrel.

HATS, HAIRCUTS AND TATTOOS

The coach is weighing his options.

His team has a tough matchup ahead, so he decides he's going to switch up some schemes to disrupt the opponent's rhythm.But when the game starts, the constant shifting only throws off his own players. They aren't clear about whom they're coming in for, they're not used to playing together, and they look entirely lost.

The coach's choice to mix up his substitutions is an example of what best-selling author James Clear considers a "haircut decision." According to Clear, there are really three types of decisions, and whatever leadership capacity we're in, we'd benefit from knowing the distinctions:

1. Hats

- Low-cost choices
- You can make a poor one with few consequences
- Move quickly and don't overthink these

Example: Choosing between wearing a tie or a nice sweater to an event.

2. Haircuts

- Mistakes that have some consequences but aren't fatal
- Our choices may make us look foolish for a short time, but will likely be forgotten
- Don't be scared of these. They're usually risks that are worth a shot

Example: Spending a lot of money on a guest speaker to address the team.

3. Tattoos

- Decisions with long-term repercussions
- Irreversible choices that can haunt us for years to come
- Should be made deliberately and with careful calculation

Example: Quitting our job and sending a scathing resignation letter to the boss.

Whether we're coaches, executives, or in another leadership position, it's important to remember that not all of our decisions should be given equal weight.

Have fun with the hats. Weigh the haircuts. And give extra consideration to the tattoos.

THE PROBLEM WITH 'SHAPING' DECISIONS

An artist shapes the painting to present the image from the mind to the canvas. A sculptor spends most of the day shaping the clay to conform to the project's vision. A musician shapes the sounds to make it pleasing to hear.

Creative people spend time shaping, as shaping is part of their process, allowing a free flow of thoughts and ideas to manifest. Shaping regarding data collection cannot be part of the decision-making process.

In 2020, for example, the San Francisco 49ers made a bold choice, trading highly-valuable assets to springboard from the 12th pick in the NFL Draft to the third.

With this aggressive move, the team intended to secure its future quarterback and find the perfect player capable of making the team a Super Bowl contender each season. The Niners claim they didn't have a predisposed idea of whom they would pick; they only knew being high in the draft would give them the flexibility to make the right decision.

Some organization members began to "shape" the information as they collected data to meet their conclusions. Shaping occurs when those responsible for curating the data begin to slant, edit and embellish to reach a predetermined decision.

This isn't a form of bias but rather an honest attempt to do what they (the staff) believe is correct. Many staffers feel since they have done the data collection, they are more informed and intune to make the correct decision over the main decision maker. When this occurs, the leader is no longer leading, and the staff is now in charge.

Shaping occurs in all organizations and can be the main cause of failure. As the chief decision-maker, the leader must understand shaping, guard against filtered data, and have a system to prevent staffers from mingling the data.

When those trusted to bring unfiltered data to the decision-makers begin to reframe the data, then shaping occurs, and bad decisions soon follow. You might argue that those collecting merely give their opinions based on their logically well-intended assessment.

Perhaps, but when you are in a "data collection phase," any conclusions cannot be reached, or else intentional shaping begins to occur. The purity of data must remain until all the evidence is declared.

A judge in the middle of hearing a case, without one side presenting, could never be allowed to make a final ruling. A judge is trained to never begin with the end in mind and understand how each attorney is "shaping" their information. Judges are trained to look past shaping, and so should all decision-makers.

We must educate those responsible to guard against shaping data. A leader ultimately making decisions must always look for shaped data. It comes in the form of a rehearsed presentation or the inability of the presenter to reverse engineer the decision.

Had the 49ers gathered information, they would've asked themselves: Why would this decision fail, as opposed to why is this decision the best? They would have avoided a mistake and understood shaping was in place.

3 RULES OF SIMPLICITY

When viewing the Sistine Chapel, it's hard to imagine that Michelangelo painted his incredible work of art using only seven colors.

When you listen to Beethoven, it's impossible to believe he achieved musical perfection with just seven notes.

Ernest Hemingway had four simple rules for writing: use short sentences, use short first paragraphs, use vigorous English, and be positive, not negative. For Hemingway, simple was always better.

Warren Buffett and Charlie Munger say, "We have a passion for keeping things simple."

We tend to believe solving a hard problem or creating something extraordinary requires complexity. We often conclude that simple and complex cannot work together, so we ignore common sense and the obvious answer.

But what separates most successful people is their ability to streamline their decision-making and creative process. They always return to the basic principles that have governed their personal and professional life.

Simplification really comes down to three rules:

Rule 1: Understand what you want to achieve.

When Michelangelo and Beethoven began their creative processes, they always took the time to decide what they were actually trying to achieve. They understood the variables they faced and what strengths they possessed to offset any problems.

Rule 2: Understand what matters most.

As leaders, coaches, teachers, or students, we might be on a downward trend at the moment. We might feel we've fallen short of our goals. To get back on track, we must understand the essentials of what creates success and work hard to improve in those specific areas. Using seven colors or notes mattered, and Beethoven and Michelangelo worked simply to create their masterpieces.

Rule 3: Understand the clutter gets in the way.

Not all information is good information. Understanding the key data points will allow you to ignore information that is only in the way.

As Steve Jobs once said: "Simple can be harder than complex: You have to work hard to get your thinking clean to make it simple. But it's worth it in the end because once you get there, you can move mountains."

Beethoven, Michelangelo, Warren Buffett, Ernest Hemingway, and Jobs were all simple, and yet they moved mountains.

You can too.

WHAT DO THEY KNOW THAT I DON'T?

The phone rings in Charlie Bluhdorn's office inside the Gulf Western Building in Midtown Manhattan.

Bluhdorn's secretary tells him that Jack Warner, founder of Warner Bros. motion pictures, is on the other line. Bluhdorn also owns Paramount Studios and competes directly with Warner Bros. for movies.

After a few pleasantries, Warner offers Bluhdorn $1 million for the rights to a book titled *The Godfather*. Bluhdorn remains poised, not overly eager, even as he calculates the profits in his head and informs Warner he will need to get back to him on his offer. Before hanging up the phone, Bluhdorn asks one simple question:

"What does Warner know about *The Godfather* that I don't know?"

Bluhdorn knows Warner is smart, savvy, and a great businessman, and doesn't toss around a million dollars for no reason. Warner has an edge, even though Bluhdorn owns the rights. Bluhdorn needs to get better informed before he decides to return the call.

If we went through life asking this one simple question, we would improve our decision-making. We would also learn more about something we think we already know.

Not every time we ask the question will we find new answers or solve new problems. But it will allow us to view something in a different mindset, a learning mindset that enables growth.

When Bill Belichick, for example, drafted Cole Strange in the first round of the NFL Draft, everyone covering the selection became negative about it, claiming it was too high, that Strange had no value, and would have been available later. No one treated Belichick like Warner. No one asked what Belichick knew that they didn't.

Everyone claimed Belichick wasn't above being criticized and that he needed to hear the rough feedback. But why wouldn't anyone react as Bluhdorn did?

The answer is, in large part, that we have stopped having an open mindset, and that ultimately prevents us from growing.

Next time something occurs far from your agreement, remind yourself of Charlie and ask the Bluhdorn question.

It might just be the best question you ask all day.

THE NFL DRAFT AND 'PREFERENCE FALSIFICATION'

If you Google "NFL Mock Draft," nearly five million results pop up in less than a second. NFL fans are infatuated with the event that began accidentally in 1958.

Bob Kelley, then the voice of the Los Angeles Rams and a longtime radio personality, wrote that after the draft, which was held in January, the team immediately started looking toward the following year.

"Then, in June, the Rams will stage a 'mock draft,'" Kelley explained. "They will pretend they are going into a regular draft meeting and will rate, in order, the top 300 players in the country."

From that simple exercise, the mock draft craze was born.

Every year the NFL holds its scouting convention, "draftniks" from all over will watch, review, and fine-tune their predictions. Their influence might appear small, but surprisingly, they hold some power over the decision-making process of NFL teams.

Timur Kuran is not a draftnik. He's a Duke University professor who developed a cognitive bias theory called preference falsification, which refers to the act of misrepresenting private beliefs in public.

Kuran's theory applies directly to decision-making in the social media era. Thoughts and behaviors are often shaped by the discomfort of holding a minority opinion and the pressure to conform in a group setting.

In essence, if a mock draft projects a player as a top-10 pick, even if a team doesn't see the same level of talent, the external noise can create doubt. The franchise, instead of trusting its own evaluation, may conform to the overwhelming "non-professional consensus."

HIRING

In his book Private Truths, Public Lies: The Social Consequences of Preference Falsification, Kuran writes that when faced with social pressure, real or perceived, people often "deliberately project a contrived opinion."

This dynamic plays out in draft rooms across the country, and it can derail the chances of a successful draft.

Why does this happen? One of the main reasons, Kuran argues, is a lack of reliable information. Without clarity, "the only sensible reaction" often feels like conformity.

Teams fall into this trap because they haven't put in the work, or they fail to ask the critical question: "What do they know that we don't?"

The only remedy is rigorous preparation. Cross-check the facts. Trust no one else's evaluation more than your own. Work harder to gather, test, and validate the right information.

Selecting talent requires leaders who not only recognize their biases but also work relentlessly to prevent those biases from clouding the process.

Because when it comes to building a team, or an organization, being on the side of the majority isn't always the right solution.

THE BATTLE OF INATTENTIONAL BLINDNESS

Former Yankees player and manager Yogi Berra once said, "You can see a lot from looking." But there are times even when we're looking where we miss something, where we fail to notice a detail, large or small. We don't mean to miss it, it just happens because we are not expecting to find what we are not ready to see. This is referred to as "inattentional blindness."

The most famous experiment on the subject, conducted by DJ Simons and C.F. Chabris, showed participants two teams playing basketball. One was dressed in white, the other in black. The people watching the video were told to count how many times the team in white passed the ball. Midway through the video, however, a gorilla walked onto the court, beat his chest, and then walked off.

At the end, viewers totaled the number of passes, ranging from 14 to 17. But over half of the research group never saw the gorilla, and were even convinced it never appeared on the screen. Even when they watched the replay, they were still skeptical and suggested that the gorilla had been spliced in later.

The study demonstrates that too often, we get caught up in the details and only find what we're looking for, not what's actually out there. As the old saying goes, "We cannot see the forest for the trees." We hear the noise, and we lose sight of the signal.

So how do we avoid "inattentional blindness"?

We must never set boundaries for what we examine. Once we narrow the focus, we miss too much.

Don't define the problem. When we ask a narrow question, we focus on a narrow answer.

Always ask, what did we miss? Never focus only on the main subject, always consider what is overlooked.

Always consider a plan B before making a decision. Working on the alternative solution forces us to broaden our perspective.

Slow down. Take your time. It's never as urgent as you think.

Making a mistake is part of our decision-making process. We all learn from our mistakes.

However, making a mistake because we never saw the full picture is inexcusable. We need to be aware of inattentional blindness and plan accordingly.

We cannot let the gorilla catch us off guard.

DON'T BE OLD SCHOOL

"Old school" is a term used to describe music, art, and general cultural trends that are associated with the 20th century.

In the 20th century, popular culture was largely influenced by the advertising industry. In an era when radio and television were still in their infancy, advertisers primarily used print ads to promote products and services. The packaging of products such as Tupperware or Campbell's soup reflected this focus on old-fashioned values like family dinners and well-behaved children.

We often hear the refrain "I'm old school" when leaders are faced with new information and ideas. By saying they are "old school," it seems to imply their methods are antiquated and etched in stone.

When former Houston Texans Coach David Culley was asked about his decision-making during the game and the use of analytics during the 2021–22 season, he said:

"I know analytics has those things out there. We do have access to all of that, but I'm old school in a way that... if I'm not feeling it, we're not doing it, regardless of what that chart says."

But does being "old school" keep information from setting in? Does being old school imply:

- You would rather wash dishes than use the dishwasher?
- You would rather look at a map than use your phone for directions?
- You would rather use a rotary phone than have a cell phone?
- You would rather use a legal pad than a computer?
- You would rather send mail than email?

- You would rather pay bills by hand each month than use Venmo?
- You would rather go to the library instead of using Google?

The list could go on and on. I'm sure Culley doesn't wash dishes, has a cell phone, uses Waze when he gets lost, and will send cash via Venmo. He is only "old school" when it's convenient to his argument. All of those new advancements aren't "old school." But gaining more information is?

Look, we all understand the situation during a game will dictate decisions and that nothing is ever cut and dry. But collecting all of the information available isn't being overly progressive or revolutionary. It's being smart.

Eric Shinseki, former Chief of Staff of the United States Army, once said: "If you don't like change you're going to like irrelevance even less."

Culley and many others must embrace change and welcome information. He doesn't have to agree with the data or implement it, he only needs to consider all of his options. Leaders like Culley are in the information business, and gaining every piece of data is the only way to make the best decision in the moment.

Saying you're old school in decision-making is not being old school. It's being closed-minded.

And no leader can afford to ever close his mind.

NFL DRAFT DAY DECISIONS

San Francisco 49ers Head Coach Bill Walsh had a plan entering the 1986 draft. He wanted one of three players: Gerald Robinson from Auburn, John L. Williams from Florida, or Ronnie Harmon from Iowa.

So with five picks remaining until his selection, he sat in front of a large desk near the end of the makeshift draft room and waited. Robinson went, then Williams, and finally Harmon. Walsh needed a new plan.

Selecting talent is hard in any profession. Every year, the NFL showcases its talent search in front of a national television audience. Fans see 32 teams unveil their hard work in data collection, processing, and formulating the best decisions possible, and many are forced to abruptly make new plans. Walsh had to do so over the course of 15 minutes. When his desired players were picked, he showed no emotion, nor did he panic or make a reactionary decision.

He instead followed important steps to help redirect the men in the room he was leading.

Walsh didn't act disappointed. Yes, he lost out on his list, but he created another list with the same enthusiasm. He wanted everyone in the room to understand he was poised, in control, and not acting from desperation.

Walsh didn't demand winning in the short term. Going against conventional wisdom, he needed time to think and replan. So he made a trade with Dallas, then with Buffalo, moving down in the draft slightly below market value. This accomplished two things: it gave him more assets in the short term while keeping him in a position to select the next player he wanted, Larry Roberts from Alabama. Walsh was more interested in winning the day, not the hour.

Walsh replanned. He identified his strengths and weaknesses of the moment, then formulated a new plan. With more picks than initially thought, Walsh needed more candidates for selection. So in the middle of the draft, with teams selecting, Walsh held a meeting to re-evaluate which players now qualified. His focus was redirected to the new task.

Walsh correctly evaluated his evaluators. When working on the new plan, he understood opinions would be overflowing and often wrong. He knew who offered the best advice.

Walsh maintained his commitment to the new plan with the same enthusiasm as the old. He kept the wind at his back and regained control. His confidence became infectious.

For a day that started poorly, it ended with one of the finest drafts in NFL history. The 49ers obtained eight starters who would go on to help the team win Super Bowls.

Most of the players selected were never discussed in detail or as part of his original plan. But by following these important steps and not falling in love with one plan, Walsh made history on this day.

We have all seen our initial plans fall apart, but how we react and redirect determines the overall outcome.

It's never about how we start.

It is always about how we finish.

LET'S NOT ANCHOR OUR DECISIONS

Sir Roger Tichborne spent several days and nights sailing around the South Atlantic Ocean off the coast of Brazil as he awaited passage to Jamaica in 1854. Tichborne was without a passport and needed to get back to France to see his mother, Lady Tichborne.

Finally, he was granted a spot on the Bella ship, which set sail for Jamaica in April of that year. But just days after leaving Rio de Janeiro, the wrecked boat was discovered off the Brazilian coast with no personnel. Bella had apparently encountered rough seas and capsized. Lady Tichborne was shocked and devastated upon receiving the news. But she never gave up hope that her son was alive. In fact, an Australian ship had picked up passengers of the Bella and transported them to Australia.

Lady Tichborne decided to be proactive. She placed advertisements in newspapers all over the world, offering a handsome reward for knowledge of her son's whereabouts. Twelve years later, she was contacted by an attorney in Australia who confirmed that Roger Tichborne was, in fact, alive and well with an entire family. Sir Roger ultimately arrived in England, and he was received by Lady Tichborne. Or so it seemed.

Many in the family were skeptical that Sir Roger was the real Sir Roger. The new Roger had different color eyes, no tattoos, was shorter in height, and had gained significant weight. All the evidence suggested that this man who'd arrived from Australia with his family was not the real Sir Roger but an imposter. Still, Lady Tichborne refused to believe it. Only after her death did the family prove that she had been clinging to false hope.

Why do we as leaders sometimes ignore undeniable facts? Why do we overlook valuable information and believe something is right even when the facts say otherwise?

We have a significant tendency to "trust our gut instincts," since our instincts have never let us down. But next time we feel as though we're relying on our instincts, let's do the following:

Acknowledge our bias. Face the fact that we are ignoring facts and choosing instead to believe in our memory or gut instincts. Research has proven our memories often are not as reliable as we might think.

Delay any decision. Take more time to review all the information and walk away. Clear your head and wait.

Drop another anchor. Take the position against what you believe and write down three reasons why your new position could be right.

We all know Lady Tichborne wanted to believe the news her son was not dead, so any information presented before her would have been overlooked. She is an extreme case.

However, had she followed these three steps, she may have avoided looking foolish. Next time your gut tells you it's right when all the evidence says it's not, let's remind ourselves of Lady Tichborne.

NFL VACANCIES AND THE 37 PERCENT RULE

At the end of every season, several NFL organizations are usually in the process of hiring new coaches and general managers. Typically, they'll create a long list of candidates, then begin interviews. After an extensive first round, they'll bring back the top two or three before making a final decision.

The process seems logical enough, but is it really that effective if six to eight head coaches of the 32 NFL teams are terminated after each season?

Franchises may benefit from considering a famous mathematics puzzle from the 1960s known as The Secretary Problem. In essence, if they're interviewing a group of applicants, how do they maximize the chances of hiring the single best? The challenge ultimately isn't who should be chosen for a position, but rather how many people should be interviewed before a final decision is reached.

Mathematicians concluded that to resolve The Secretary Problem, employers needed to decide on either the total number of applicants they wanted to interview or the length of time they wanted to interview applicants for.

Whichever path is agreed to then requires two additional steps: the look and then the leap.

The Look Phase
Organizations interview a wide range of candidates without making any decisions. They then narrow their list to only 37 percent of the possibilities (typically three out of eight).

The Leap Phase
Instead of settling for one of those initial three, they begin another round of interviews with entirely different people,

hoping to find someone better. If they do, that person is the one they must hire.

Most teams adhere to the look phase but fail to get into the leap stage where they could potentially find a better match. It's a common challenge for so many of us. We make rash decisions, quickly selecting what we feel is the best option without considering that there could be other possibilities. Then, when our selection doesn't pan out, we grow frustrated and wonder where we went wrong.

By establishing the 37 percent rule, though, we set in place an acceptable standard of excellence, then strive for more in hopes of ultimately discovering the best.

When a profession loses one-quarter of its workforce annually, there is a major problem.

Perhaps the 37 percent rule can help solve it.

HOW BIASED ARE YOUR DECISIONS?

In his highly acclaimed book *Seeking Wisdom: From Darwin to Munger,* author Peter Bevelin provides a ground-breaking analysis of why we, at times, make poor decisions.

Bevelin focuses deeply on bias, how our internal prejudices factor into our decision-making. He breaks down bias into 28 distinct types, some extremely common, some not as much. Yet each impacts our ability to make rational judgments. Here are the top 5 biases Bevelin describes:

Mere-Association Bias
This occurs when we see situations as identical because they appear similar to something we've experienced. We often try to compare situations to help us streamline our decisions, yet we frequently end up comparing an apple to an orange, which then results in a poor choice.

Confirmation Bias
We're more familiar with this one. We begin with the end in mind, believing that we must be right and collecting only the data that supports our initial hypothesis.

Bias from Over-Influence
We like the person giving us the information, therefore we don't question the information. We simply trust the person who provided it and do not take the time to gather the facts on our own.

Bias from Anchoring
This occurs when we cling to one or two items that anchor our thoughts and beliefs, even if those two points might not be totally relevant to the bigger picture.

Bias from Social Proof
This occurs when we just go with popular opinion to be liked and accepted by the masses. We become

influenced by what everyone else says and don't take time to think independently.

Next time we're forced to make a tough decision, let's commit to making sure we're not committing any of these inherent biases. Let's commit to drawing our own independent conclusions, regardless of how many people may say otherwise.

WE MUST ELIMINATE PLAN CONTINUATION BIAS

Catholic school nuns loved to teach the concept of "sticktoitiveness." They wanted their students not to give up, to stay the course, to always finish what they started. It was a common theme that became ingrained in daily behavior. But was it good? Is being so rigid in our behavior helping us? Should we always finish a book we start even if we don't enjoy it? Should we always stay the course and not change even though it's wrong?

The Torrey Canyon Tanker was one of the largest vessels of its time, carrying more than 119,000 tons of crude oil, bound for Cornwall, England. Because of the rough seas and current, the boat was pulled off course and needed to navigate around the deadly reef known as the Seven Stones. Captain Pastrengo Rugiati was a regimented man who always followed protocols. When notified the ship was off course, Rugiati decided to stick with his original plan because he did not want to risk a two-hour delay waiting for the right tides to deliver his crude oil on time. Rugiati was slow to adjust even though everyone on the ship knew he was heading for those deadly rocks.

What Rugiati did is known as "plan continuation bias." The bias occurs when people stick to the plan even if the plan appears wrong. Now, you might say that sounds ridiculous; however, more often than not, once a plan is in place, any adjustment to the plan becomes a challenge, and our "sticktoitiveness" takes over. This bias often occurs in the airline industry. Airline pilots believe they can narrowly escape bad weather approaching and develop a bias called "get-there-itis." Accident investigators often believe crashes occur because of this bias, that the idea of a pause or a change of approach becomes not just aggravating, expensive or embarrassing, it becomes literally unthinkable.

Developing plans is fun, and when they work without a hitch, they make us look smart. But our skills as leaders can never be judged by the original plan. Our skills will always be judged by our ability to think quickly on our feet, to anticipate problems instead of simply reacting to them, and to make quick adjustments when the time is right. Had Rugiati made one small adjustment instead of being devoted to his plan, he would not have caused the largest oil spill in the North Atlantic.

Sticking to something shows persistence. Changing on the go shows intelligence. Smart always wins.

BUS DRIVER PLAYERS

Bill Walsh, former Hall of Fame coach of the San Francisco 49ers, would stand before his players on the first day of training camp and tell them:

"It doesn't matter where you were drafted or how much money you were given. It only matters how you play from this moment forward."

Walsh believed deeply in meritocracy. He wanted everyone to earn their place, not to be handed one based on status or history. Building a team rooted in meritocracy requires a leader to remove bias and ego from decision-making. It also demands a willingness to teach and to resist settling for people who know what to do but can no longer do it.

On every team, some individuals earn their roles through performance, while others earn them through knowledge, essentially serving as extensions of the coach. These players inspire confidence because of their reliability. Walsh called them "Bus Driver Players." Unless they were on the bus, the driver wouldn't know how to get to the stadium. They knew the route by heart and the team couldn't function without them.

But knowing what to do and executing it are never the same. Once a leader decides that knowledge outweighs ability, the foundation of meritocracy begins to crumble. True leadership requires balancing experience with talent.

Developing a merit-based team requires foresight, patience, and courage, the willingness to sacrifice short-term wins for long-term growth. Walsh often told his staff he would rather lose a game early in the season playing a young player than win one with an older, declining veteran. He understood that older players fade over time, while younger ones improve with experience.

HIRING

He also knew that assistant coaches would naturally lean toward Bus Driver Players because they made their jobs easier. If the team failed, they could point to a lack of talent rather than coaching.

Walsh refused to let that mindset take root. He preached true meritocracy and made sure no Bus Driver Players ever got onto his bus.

ONBOARD

STORIES ON ONBOARDING

TAKE YOURSELF ON: THE LEADERSHIP LESSON EVERY NEW HIRE NEEDS

Simon Sinek, a renowned author and motivational speaker, is celebrated for his groundbreaking ideas on leadership and organizational culture. Best known for his concept of "Start with Why," Sinek emphasizes the importance of purpose-driven leadership. And when it comes to onboarding new hires, he shares two simple but powerful principles that capture his philosophy on work and life.

Sinek personally calls every new employee of his company and tells them two things. First, "Welcome. You're now part of something bigger than yourself. Our little company influences millions of people around the world, and your work will impact many."

Second, he tells them he expects they will "take yourself on."

That principle, "take yourself on," reflects Sinek's belief that personal growth and self-improvement have to start from within. He believes every employee should have a hunger to make self-improvement a top priority every single day. His challenge to new hires is simple: focus on becoming a better version of yourself every day, and let that personal growth fuel your professional journey. It's about continuous learning, self-awareness, and committing to personal excellence.

The first step in aligning personal and professional growth is realizing the importance of your role in something bigger. As Sinek reminds his new hires, being part of an organization means you have the chance to contribute to something beyond yourself. That perspective creates purpose and a sense of belonging, and it motivates you to perform not just for personal success, but to make a real difference. And the truth is, "taking yourself on" isn't a selfish journey. It's how you strengthen the entire team.

Take time to reflect on how your work connects to the organization's mission and values. Ask yourself: How does my role contribute to the company's bigger goals? What unique skills and strengths do I bring to the team? How can my personal growth help make a bigger impact here?

Answering these questions helps you see how personal excellence and collective success go hand in hand.

Sinek's philosophy is a reminder that personal development isn't separate from the work you do, it's directly tied to it. Yes, work on yourself. But also pay attention to how your growth improves the people and culture around you. Collaboration, empathy, and inspiring others are just as important as individual achievement.

At the end of the day, alignment happens when your personal passions and professional goals connect. Find ways to bring your interests and values into the work you do.

For example: If you're passionate about creativity, look for ways to innovate in your role. If you value mentorship, be the person who guides and supports your colleagues. If sustainability matters to you, champion eco-friendly practices at work.

Aligning personal growth with your professional journey is an ongoing process. It takes intentionality, self-awareness, and a daily commitment to getting better. And as Sinek says, take yourself on, make self-improvement a priority and embrace the journey of becoming your best self. When you do, you'll elevate not just your career, but the lives of the people around you.

MANAGING DAY 1 OF NFL TRAINING CAMP

Each NFL season begins as all 32 teams report to training camp full of hope, optimism, and expectation. Slightly fewer than 3,000 players will battle for roster spots in hopes of fulfilling the dream of competing on fall Sundays in the NFL.

One of the hardest jobs for any leader at the beginning of a new year filled with excitement is to manage the organization's and the players' expectations. Most want to rush to the finish line without taking the vital steps along the way to ensure the proper foundation of success. There is a permeating belief that the organization worked hard in the off-season and added more talent, so naturally, success will be right around the corner.

It becomes easy to jump ahead. Players worry about making the team, worry about how many reps they get in practice, and where they appear on the depth chart. And it becomes next to impossible to stay in the moment because the fans, the media, and constant coverage create huge expectations down the road.

From day one, the head coach must talk ONLY about day one, not the first pre-season game, when the pads come on, or the first regular-season opponent. Day one sets the tone, and the leader can never allow the group to look past it. He must urge the players to take advantage of every single rep they receive, focusing on doing the best they can with what they're given on that day. The coach must continue to emphasize that players control the controllables, their hydration, lifting, mental preparation, and most of all, their overall health.

Teaching players to stay in the moment is as vital as any play in the playbook, so many successful coaches begin their first practice with rudimentary drills. By going back to the basics, the leader emphasizes the current moment and keeps everyone present by performing a simple task.

The psychologist Abraham Maslow once said, "The ability to be in the present moment is a major component of mental wellness."

Staying in the moment will be a central theme throughout the long season, and teaching the organization how to do this is the No. 1 job of the leader.

By reinforcing that each day is the only day, each drill and each play is all that matters, the momentum of being present builds and becomes part of the team's DNA. It also eliminates any unrealistic expectations that can quickly derail a season.

Let the media talk about the future. We as leaders need to talk about the only day that matters: TODAY.

RULES FOR TALENT

The Antonio Brown saga dominated sports news for years. Much of the story centered on erratic behavior and social media outbursts. The Oakland Raiders took a calculated risk, spending money and draft capital to acquire the talented yet volatile wide receiver. Buying low allowed the Raiders to convince themselves they could make the problems disappear, that a change of scenery would enable Brown to return to form on the field.

From day one, Antonio Brown was a massive headache. From skipping offseason workouts to complaining about his helmet, to frostbitten feet and constant distractions, Brown brought more chaos than production.

What can we learn from this fiasco?

First and foremost, leaders must confront the illusion that they can change people, especially uniquely talented people. Ego often convinces us otherwise. We believe our skills as leaders can fix what's missing in a "risky" employee's life. But when ego takes over, we stop observing behavior objectively and begin personalizing the problem.

Here are some principles to help navigate talented but volatile individuals:

1. Set the Expectations, Be Honest

Communicate clearly before the hiring process, leaving no ambiguities. Lay out the plan in detail and explain it directly to the individual. Never rely on others to speak on behalf of the organization. Involve their representatives if necessary, but always be direct, honest, and transparent. When taking on risks, leadership cannot carry the burden alone, the individual and their circle must be equally accountable.

2. Provide Behavioral Feedback

Daily feedback is essential. Direct and immediate input, whether positive or negative, helps ensure clarity. People tend to behave better when they know they are being observed and evaluated consistently.

3. Be Consistent

Once rules are set, they must be enforced without exception. There can be no blurred lines, no second chances, and no misinterpretations. Consistency builds trust within the organization and prevents culture erosion.

4. Establish Consequences

Create a clear plan of action for when expectations are violated. Accountability delayed is accountability denied, and postponing consequences can poison the culture of the entire team.

5. Have Courage

Don't let talent fool you. As Bill Parcells famously said, "When someone shows you who they are, believe them." Don't make excuses or fear negative publicity. Always do what's best for the team. Winning and culture matter more than optics.

EFFORT VS. EXCELLENCE: WHAT REALLY MATTERS

When a carpenter shows up to work each day, they bring their tools, an assortment of items, from a hammer and nails to a drill and measuring tape, all wrapped around their waist for easy access. On their tool belt are the essentials needed to perform the job correctly and effectively.

The same holds true for the barber, the plumber, the roofer, or any craftsperson who relies on their hands to make a living. When students walk into class, they bring notebooks, laptops, pens, and pencils, tools that help them take notes, capture ideas, and curate information from their teacher. But before a grade is given, the student must turn those notes into knowledge, proving their comprehension.

The carpenter and the student both work hard. Yet their effort isn't judged. Their finished product is.

How many times have you interviewed someone for a position, only to hear their first selling point is their ability to work hard? Hard work and persistence aren't tools in a candidate's belt, they're a given. They're not a bonus. They don't distinguish one candidate from another. Everyone needs to work hard. Everyone needs persistence. What matters more than effort are results, for the laborer, the student, and the professional alike.

In an opinion piece for *The New York Times*, Adam Grant addressed the issue of treating effort as if it were gradable:

"After 20 years of teaching, I thought I'd heard every argument in the book from students who wanted a better grade. But at the end of a weeklong course with a light workload, multiple students had a new complaint: 'My grade doesn't reflect the effort I put into this course.'

High marks are for excellence, not grit. In the past, students understood that hard work was not sufficient; an A required great work. Yet today, many students expect to be rewarded for the quantity of their effort rather than the quality of their knowledge. In surveys, two-thirds of college students say that 'trying hard' should be a factor in their grades, and a third think they should get at least a B just for showing up to (most) classes."

This begs the question: when did the paradigm shift? At what point did we begin equating effort with excellence?

The truth is that in any professional or academic setting, results are what matter most. Hard work, while necessary, is only the baseline expectation. The differentiator is the output, the quality of the work, the innovation, the execution, the impact.

In the workforce, employers don't hire people simply to try hard. They hire people who deliver. Projects aren't completed by sheer willpower; they require knowledge, skill, and consistent follow-through. Similarly, in academia, students are expected to demonstrate mastery through their exams, papers, and projects, not simply through attendance and participation.

Elevating effort to the same level as achievement dilutes the value of true excellence. Hard work should be the foundation upon which we build skills and accomplishments, not the pinnacle of our aspirations.

In a world where effort is expected from everyone, it's results that set us apart.

LEVEL 5 LEADERSHIP: THE JOURNEY FROM GOOD TO GREAT

Leadership isn't something you can opt out of. Whether you realize it or not, you are leading in some facet of your life.

The question isn't if you're a leader, it's whether you're an effective one.

This brings us to a bigger question: Can the highest form of leadership, Level 5 Leadership, be developed?

In business expert Jim Collins' book *Good to Great*, he identifies five distinct levels of leadership. While most people stop or plateau at Level 4, leaders who reach the pinnacle of Level 5 have a unique blend of personal humility and indomitable will.

They aren't just about achieving goals; they're relentlessly focused on a cause larger than themselves. Their ambition is deeply tied to the organization, the team, the mission, and the people they serve.

Level 1: Highly Capable Individual – Makes productive contributions through talent, knowledge, skills, and good work habits.

Level 2: Contributing Team Member – Contributes to the achievement of group objectives; works effectively with others in a group setting.

Level 3: Competent Manager – Organizes people and resources toward the effective and efficient pursuit of predetermined objectives.

Level 4: Effective Leader – Catalyzes commitment to and vigorous pursuit of a clear and compelling vision; stimulates the group to high performance standards.

Level 5: Executive Leadership – Builds enduring greatness through a paradoxical combination of personal humility and professional will.

Whether you're at the beginning of your leadership journey or already climbing the ladder, consider these questions: Where do you currently stand in the hierarchy? What steps can you take to evolve and level up? Are you prepared to channel your personal ambitions into something greater than yourself? Can you cultivate humility alongside your drive for success?

Leadership is not about reaching a destination; it's about evolving. Whether you are at Level 1 or nearing Level 5, each stage presents a unique opportunity to reflect, learn, and improve.

The question isn't just whether leadership can be learned. The real question is whether you have the resolve and resilience to become a more effective and transformational leader, and reach Level 5.

IT AIN'T A HALLOWEEN COSTUME: THE DAILY DISCIPLINE OF WINNING

In today's fast-paced world of leadership and high performance, it's easy to become consumed by metrics, quarterly results, and endgame outcomes. But true, lasting success isn't forged in the final moments, it's built in the daily habits, the invisible decisions, and the quiet hours when no one is watching.

Few articulate this better than Duke University's Women's Basketball Coach, Kara Lawson. While her title says "Head Coach," her mission goes far beyond wins and losses on the basketball court. She's a teacher, a mentor, and a transformational leader, educating not only her players but also a global audience that tunes into her social media channels for life lessons rooted in leadership, culture-building, and personal transformation.

Coach Lawson understands something many leaders miss: she isn't just preparing her team for the next rep, practice, or game, she's preparing them for the most important game of all... life. She knows her true calling is to help shape people who perform at a high level long after the final buzzer sounds.

In a powerful message shared on social media, Coach Lawson warned her team of a silent but deadly threat: losing habits.

"Once you develop losing habits, they're hard to get out," she told her team.

"That's the problem with losing habits, once they infiltrate this circle, they're hard to kill. So we have to stop them before they become habits. And I'm going to tell you every time I see it, but then it's incumbent upon you to stop it within yourself. You have to practice and play and behave like a winner. If you want to win games, you have to do that.

It's not something you just decide to be when you wake up. It ain't a Halloween costume. You can't just wake up and put it on. You have to be that every single day in your approach and execution."

That line hits hard: "It ain't a Halloween costume." This isn't just a message for athletes, it's a powerful call to action for all of us navigating the complex arenas of leadership and life.

We may not win every game, every deal, every quarter, or every opportunity we pursue. But that's not the point. What matters is the mentality behind our approach to the craft, the pursuit, and the lives we lead. It's about showing up with integrity, intention, accountability, and an unrelenting commitment to doing the hard and uncomfortable things, consistently.

In a culture of convenience, where the thrill of winning seems deliverable at the tap of a button and validation arrives in likes and clicks, it's easy to become complacent. But the winner's mentality isn't forged in comfort. It's forged in the relentless pursuit of excellence, in the refusal to settle, and in the daily decision to prepare and perform with greater purpose, regardless of the scoreboard, regardless of who is watching.

Coach Lawson's words remind us that winning isn't an outcome, it's a way of life.

So ask yourself: What's my daily standard, even when no one's watching? Where might I be developing quiet losing habits, cutting corners, lowering standards, or avoiding the hard conversations?

How can I change the narrative and recommit to a winner's mentality in those areas?

Each of us was born to win. It's our birthright. But somewhere along the way, life's disappointments and failures whisper that we don't belong, that we're not capable or worthy. Let's not internalize that lie.

Remember: A true winner doesn't just celebrate the victories. They find power even in the losses, because their identity isn't tied to outcomes; it's tethered to the process. And that process, practiced daily, leads to a life of impact, fulfillment, inner excellence, and deeper meaning.

Coach Lawson's challenge is clear: Don't just try to win, be a winner. Every day. In your mentality, your habits, your actions. Because the truth is, we don't just coach or lead others, we're coaching and leading ourselves, too.

TAKING OVER A TOXIC WORKPLACE

Josh Harris, the leading partner of the Washington Commanders, spent over $6 billion to inherit a teardown.

He bought a once-proud franchise with a 20-year season ticket waiting list that was systematically destroyed by its former narcissistic owner, Daniel Snyder.

Replacing Snyder will be viewed positively and allow Harris to bask in the sunshine for a brief moment. But once he removes his coat and enters his new workspace, he will learn the mess is bigger than he could have imagined.

Since Snyder purchased the team in 1999, his horrible leadership style and poor behavior have been ingrained throughout the organization. Though employees have come and gone, the scars remain.

A toxic culture never immediately vanishes with a simple changing of the guard. It lingers, hiding in small places.

Removing those scars won't be easy. It will take time, supreme effort, and most of all, it will require Harris to prove his trustworthiness.

Before changes can occur, Harris must gain a true understanding of the deep-rooted issues of the franchise and learn these himself; he can't simply rely on others to "bring him up to speed."

The "bringing up to speed" method for any leader is risky. It relies on the evaluator being correct when the leader typically hasn't "evaluated the evaluator." If the evaluator is wrong, this shortcut proves to be a major waste of time, and time is of the essence here.

Almost every new leader enters with a 100-day plan, a new direction and vision created from afar, mostly by those involved. But how can the leader know the path without truly understanding the real issues?

For Harris to develop trust and understanding of the central concerns, he must announce to all, in a fully transparent manner, that he will spend the next few months collecting data from those in the entire organization, from the cleaning services to the president.

A leader cannot develop complete trust when there is the potential for bias, and relying on the evaluations of those in the building regarding others could easily destroy his intentions of building a new culture.

To rebuild the culture properly, Harris cannot allow bias to creep into his decision-making. When people in the organization see Harris acting independently, they will trust his decisions. If they see him relying on the former top brass, they won't.

In taking over a toxic culture, Harris needs to demonstrate fairness, let the employees speak for themselves, and not rely on what others might believe.

Every employee believes he or she knows the problems and how to quickly repair the team, only from their perspective and their self-interest.

Most will blame Snyder. But while pointing the finger at him for all of the problems is easy, it will never allow Harris to fully understand what he needs to do to establish the culture.

Digging deep, independently spending time around everyone, observing, and listening are the only ways he can dig himself out of the mess he just purchased.

Harris must be the culture changer and the instrument of change.

Only he can return the franchise to its days of greatness.

HIRING

HOW COACH K COMMANDED THE ROOM

The coach didn't belong. It was July of 2006, and many of the best American basketball players were assembled in a hotel room in Las Vegas, superstars from rival NBA franchises attempting to restore glory to Team USA, which had been embarrassed in recent years.

But the man tasked with leading them had no NBA experience and coached at a college several of them grew up despising.

So, how did Mike Krzyzewski command respect? How does a leader who appears to be an outsider win over an audience that may be skeptical?

Coach K did three things in particular, featured in the Redeem Team Netflix documentary, that are relevant to anyone trying to win the room.

1. Create the cause

Krzyzewski didn't mince words in his first meeting. He spoke tersely but respectfully, using colorful language that established a firm and authoritative tone. "In order to win a fight, you have to know who you're fighting," he said. "You're fighting somebody who thinks they're Superman. They have nothing to lose."

It was a humbling message intended to establish an underdog mentality among a group used to the highest levels of success. But it struck a chord and established a pervasive attitude for the entire group. Ultimately, it sparked crucial buy-in.

2. Speak to, not at

Coach K was masterful in making realistic demands. He didn't scream at the world's greatest players to lose their identities and make peace with terrible stats or low minutes. He just asked them to sacrifice a bit and unite over a period of time.

"You have to give me the egos that you have on your current basketball team, bring them to this team, and put them all under one ego umbrella," he said. Once again, it was an in-touch demand, and players could understand the logic behind it.

3. **Find alternative messengers**

    Krzyzewski consistently preached the values of unity and sacrifice, but any team will get tired of solely hearing a single voice.

    So, he brought in U.S. Army personnel who were also able to speak to the importance of representing a nation and the selfless service required to accomplish a daunting task.

    We may not have the budget to bring in guests, but as leaders, we'd be wise to look for alternative ways to communicate messages we desperately want our teams to process.

Talent alone doesn't lead to success. True greatness is only attainable when a collective purpose is conveyed and standards and expectations are made abundantly clear.

Despite his prior inexperience leading generational basketball superstars, Coach K was able to establish his authority with Team USA within hours.

And his wise words on sacrifice, humility, and collective purpose can lead to gold for any leader.

THE 3 MAJOR PROBLEMS WITH INCENTIVIZING TALENT

Former NBA Coach Jeff Van Gundy once said: "Your best player has to set a tone of intolerance for anything that gets in the way of winning."

Van Gundy, like all coaches and leaders, wanted his top talent to help him establish a winning identity. When the best player works the hardest, cares the most, and complies with culture, everyone else follows.

But can an organization establish a culture when the best player doesn't prepare or work the hardest?

In 2022, Arizona Cardinals starting quarterback Kyler Murray signed a lucrative new contract worth over $230 million. In it, there was an addendum that stated: "Murray will need to study material provided to him by the club to prepare for the club's next upcoming game."

Murray would receive "credit" for completing his film study, but failure to meet the addendum requirements would mean he'd "be in default" of the contract. If that were to happen, the Cardinals could walk away without having to pay him. In essence, the team was incentivizing work habits.

So can an organization make a player who doesn't naturally work hard work harder? Do incentives like this really work? Can they help us build team culture?

Extensive research has been conducted over the years looking into motivating employees to perform at a higher level when rewards are offered. According to the Harvard Business Review: "Research suggests that, by and large, rewards succeed at securing one thing only: temporary compliance. However, rewards, like punishment, are strikingly ineffective when it comes to producing lasting change in attitudes and behavior."

Why don't rewards work, and why were these Murray incentives likely to flop?

Money doesn't change habits. Even in a case like Murray's, where the player has 230 million reasons to adjust his behavior, he likely will change in the short term, not the long. Murray already believed he was different. He told *The New York Times* in 2020: "I think I was blessed with the cognitive skills to just go out there and just see it before it happens. I'm not one of those guys that's going to sit there and kill myself watching film. I don't sit there for 24 hours and break down this team and that team and watch every game because, in my head, I see so much."

Rewards divide the culture. Why does Murray have to be treated differently? Teammates will wonder why the organization rewarded Murray with a record deal when they knew he didn't work hard. With this structure, work habits, good conduct, and team commitment are no longer seen as vital to the front office. Can the coaches now really stand in front of the team and demand hard work when they've established a double standard?

Rewards make people lazy. People with incentive-laced deals will do the work that earns them incentives, but nothing else. They lose motivation to be curious or go above and beyond. The team then fails to grow together, and everyone only cares about their individual rewards, not the ultimate prize of winning.

So ask yourself: If you have to use incentives for your best player to work and lead, then is he or she really your best player?

ARE WE UNLOCKING DOORS FOR OTHERS?

Are we door openers? Are we providing growth opportunities for others, and for ourselves?

As leaders, we have both an obligation and a social responsibility to open doors for the individual members of our teams.

Some are unlocked, and all we have to do is turn the knob. That's easy. But others are double-bolted.

We strive to get our teams to buy into our values, our habits, and our mission. But our players and employees have personal goals that lie on the other side of a locked door. And they need our help to reach them.

We need to be their locksmiths. We need to understand their vision, we need to follow up, and we need to have keys ready to unlock doors for them.

Let's make sure we ask if they know whether the space on the other side is bright or dark, large or small. Is it worth the time and effort? We don't want to waste energy prying a door open that leads to a dungeon.

Not everyone on our team will know their personal goals. That's OK. Can we recommend a door and a pathway?

As leaders, we need to realize that most of those we lead can't get to where they want to go on their own. Some don't even know what direction they're facing. If our response to that is, "I did it on my own. Why can't they?" then we're really missing it. We have to have solutions to problems and suggestions for uncertainty.

Ultimately, we will be judged by our wins and losses, our bottom line, the tangible performance indicators.

But the most pivotal part of our leadership record is the number of doors we unlock for others.

And when we help our players and employees manifest their personal dreams, we'll likely find that the doors begin to open for ourselves as well.

THE LEADERSHIP POWER OF 'YOU'RE ALLOWED TO MAKE A MISTAKE

The Marquette Golden Eagles went head-to-head with the UConn Huskies in a game filled with high expectations during the 2024-25 season. When the final buzzer sounded, UConn had secured a 77-69 victory.

But the most powerful moment of the game? It didn't come from a highlight dunk or a clutch three-pointer. It came from the sidelines, during a timeout.

Marquette's head coach, Shaka Smart, was mic'd up, and instead of delivering a fiery speech or breaking down plays, he offered his team something much deeper: a reminder to breathe.

"Let go. Relax. Tell yourself a joke. Stop taking yourself so seriously. You're allowed to make a mistake. You're so tight and wound up that you're not giving yourself a chance," Coach Smart told his team in the huddle.

In that huddle, Coach Smart wasn't just talking about basketball. He was teaching and modeling leadership.

If you've ever been in a high-pressure situation, whether in an important meeting, a big game, or a moment where everything feels like it's on the line, you know that gripping too tightly can backfire.

The more we try to force perfection, the more we hesitate. The more we overthink, the more our confidence erodes. Fear of making a mistake becomes the very thing that keeps us from performing at our best.

Coach Smart saw it in his players. They were too tense, too locked in on avoiding mistakes instead of trusting their instincts and one another. As a transformational leader, he knew his job wasn't just to coach strategy, in that moment, it was to help them release the weight of pressure so they could play more freely.

The best leaders don't just push their teams toward results; they create environments where people feel free to take risks, make mistakes, and grow. Excellence isn't about being perfect, it's about staying loose, staying prepared, staying present, and trusting ourselves.

Let's think about your own leadership style and approach: Do we lead from fear or from trust? Do we create space for people to take risks, or do we make them afraid of making mistakes? Does our fixation on perfection prevent us from leading with confidence and playing liberated?

The best teams, whether in sports, business, or life, aren't the ones that never fail. They're the ones that trust themselves enough to take chances, bounce back, and keep moving forward.

So the next time you're feeling the pressure, or you notice your team tightening up, take a page from Coach Smart's playbook: "Let go. Relax. Tell yourself a joke. You're allowed to make a mistake."

Because sometimes, that's exactly what it takes to win.

DEREK JETER ON FAILURE: 'DON'T LET THE SPEED BUMP BECOME A ROADBLOCK

Long before he stood in front of 70,000 people at Michigan Stadium as the commencement speaker, Derek Jeter was already known for something bigger than baseball. He was The Captain. A five-time World Series champion, Hall of Famer, and cultural icon, Jeter's greatness wasn't just measured in stats or titles, it was built on professionalism, poise under pressure, relentless consistency, and an unwavering team-first mentality.

He didn't just play for New York. He gave the city, and fans everywhere, belief and a blueprint for honoring the craft, showing up for the process, and giving everything you love to the game and your teammates.

The Yankees legend returned to the place where his college dreams began, briefly, before the majors came calling. Enrolled at the University of Michigan in 1992, Jeter left just a year later after being drafted by the Yankees. But standing at the Big House decades later, his message to graduates had nothing to do with batting averages or championships. It had everything to do with choices, purpose, and the courage to fail.

"How you approached today, and every day, is a choice, your choice. Your life will ultimately be framed by the choices you make," Jeter said.

In a world obsessed with perfection and success, Jeter kept it real, talking about failure not in distant, abstract terms but in vivid, personal ones.

"Failure. Failure is essential. If I can promise you one thing for certain: You will fail," he said.

"The bigger the dream, the bigger the risk. What is the price if you don't take the risk? If you don't commit to the dream? You might end up overmatched. But maybe you won't. I failed publicly. I failed miserably. There were days I literally cried because I was so bad. My first season as a professional, I made 56 errors. And for the non-baseball fans, that is hard to do intentionally... But you, me, every one of us has to learn to deal with failure. I wouldn't have had the success without the failures."

In a world that celebrates highlight reels and picture-perfect outcomes, Jeter offered something far more powerful: permission to fail, and a mandate to keep going when we do.

"It's your job to make sure that a speed bump doesn't become a roadblock."

Too often, when things don't go our way, when we suffer defeat or fall short, we start contemplating the exit ramp. We tell ourselves maybe we're not built for this. Maybe the dream was too big. Maybe it's time to quit.

But what if failure is just the beginning? What if adversity isn't a verdict, but a teacher?

"Surround yourself with the right people," Jeter added. "While you may fail on your own, it's nearly impossible to succeed alone."

For us as leaders, coaches, and high performers, this is more than motivational fluff, it's strategic wisdom. One of the greatest competitive advantages we can build, both for ourselves and our teams, is the willingness to wrestle with failure and lean into it, not retreat from it.

Because it's easy to play it safe. But are we truly living when we do? It's easy to stay comfortable. But leadership isn't about avoiding failure, it's about engaging with it. Choosing to see it not as a signal to stop, but as a moment to grow, improve, and transform.

There will be days we question ourselves. Moments that shake us to the core. Days and nights when we need to pause, cry, breathe more deeply, rest, recharge, sit in the sadness and simply be still. And that's okay. That's what makes us human. These moments allow us to fully feel the failure, but also give us a profound opportunity: to choose not to be defined by it.

It's in these moments, the ones we'd never choose, but life hands us anyway, that the true test of leading ourselves and others begins.

And it's where we must decide: Will we let the speed bump become a roadblock, or will we find a way to keep moving forward?

WINNING WITHOUT BEING DEFINED BY THE WIN

Each day is a unique opportunity to be chasing something. Yet, in that chase, balancing the demands and noise of the outside world with the internal critic of the perfectionist, our identity can become so warped in our pursuits that we lose ourselves. We put at risk our relationships, our peace, our well-being, and ultimately, our ability to find fulfillment in the process.

To reach a high level of excellence in our respective crafts requires sacrifice, resilience, hard work, and discipline, none of which are negotiable. Yet, it's a slippery slope. What we do is not all of who we are.

Tennis champion Madison Keys captured this brilliantly after finally winning her first Grand Slam title. We can achieve more, including in our careers, when we don't allow ourselves to be defined by them. Her victory was the culmination of years of effort, battling injuries, enduring crushing setbacks, and relentlessly pursuing this elusive goal.

She described the weight of chasing that dream:

"From a pretty young age, I felt like if I never won a Grand Slam, then I wouldn't have lived up to what people thought I should have been. That was a pretty heavy burden to carry around," Keys said.

Yet, Madison Keys' biggest transformation didn't just happen on the court, it happened within. She kept showing up, getting the physical reps, but just as importantly, doing the inner work.

"I've done a lot of work to no longer need this. I really wanted it, but it was no longer the thing that was going to define me. And kind of letting go of that burden, I think, finally gave myself the ability to actually play for it."

In our quietest moments of reflection, we must ask ourselves: How much of our self-worth is tied to what we do and the titles we hold? There is no right or wrong answer, only the acknowledgment that can be the birthplace of a breakthrough.

Keys' words remind us that we are not defined by our work, our accolades, or our bank accounts. We are worthy simply because we are alive.

She also puts two important themes into perspective, ones that are crucial as we think about leading ourselves and our organizations:

1. What does success truly look and feel like?
Coach John Wooden once said: "Success is peace of mind, which is a direct result of self-satisfaction in knowing you did your best to become the best that you are capable of becoming."

Many of us may have strayed far from this true definition of success. Have we lost sight of what it really means? Is success merely measured by external achievements and acquisitions, or is it found in the ongoing journey of growth and becoming?

2. Are we still having fun?
Does the process of showing up for our work, our craft, for those we lead still ignite that burning fire within us? Are we still driven by passion, or have we become consumed by pressure and expectation?

Life is short. No matter how long we live, it's fragile. Tomorrow is never guaranteed. So we must not postpone our living. We must not delay taking the leap. We must not wait to chase the things that make us feel most alive.

We should strive for greatness and mastery in our pursuits, but our identity and worth don't have to be tethered to the outcome.

The key lies in embracing the duality, dedicating ourselves to the work and striving for excellence while staying unattached to the outcome. Madison Keys embodies this mindset, and her journey has become a powerful testament to that liberation.

ACKNOWLEDGMENTS

This *Hiring* book is the product of many minds, many voices, and a shared belief that leadership is one of the greatest forms of leverage. It touches every corner of our lives, from the teams we join, to the organizations we build, to the communities we call home.

We are deeply grateful to the voices past and present whose words, insights, and lived experiences fill these pages. Their dedication to leading themselves, serving others, and making a positive difference in as many lives as possible, and their commitment to elevating leaders through ideas, questions, and lessons, has made *Hiring* possible.

To our writing contributors, thank you for lending your craft and perspective to this work. Your contributions reflect not just knowledge, but also the generosity of spirit required to teach, challenge, and inspire. Your brilliance runs throughout this project, and your impact will be felt by every reader who turns these pages.

To our broader Daily Coach community, the coaches, executives, educators, teammates, and readers, thank you for walking with us. Your trust, curiosity, and willingness to grow are the reason these words matter and why the work we do each day is so meaningful.

And finally, to you, the reader: may the insights here serve as a compass as you hire, lead, and build. May they help you see not only what a role requires, but also what a person can become and transform into when given the chance to contribute authentically and at their fullest.

OTHER WORKS BY DAILY COACH CO-FOUNDERS

Discover the inspiring books penned by our founders, where their leadership vision and expertise come to life.

What You're Made For By George Raveling and Ryan Holiday

Stories and wisdom from the pioneering basketball coach and former Nike executive George Raveling, coauthored by bestselling author of *The Daily Stoic* Ryan Holiday. Whether you're an athlete, a leader, a parent, a student, or simply seeking to mold your raw talent into greatness, *What You're Made For* is a blueprint for your life.

Gridiron Genius by Michael Lombardi

Former NFL general manager and three-time Super Bowl winner Michael Lombardi reveals what makes football organizations tick at the championship level. From personnel to practice to game-day decisions that win titles, Lombardi shares what he learned working with coaching legends Bill Walsh of the 49ers, Al Davis of the Raiders, and Bill Belichick of the Patriots, among others, during his three decades in football.

Football Done Right by Michael Lombardi

Michael Lombardi takes readers on the ultimate journey through the NFL's history to present his calls on the greatest players and coaches the sport has ever seen.

War On The Boards by George Raveling

Never before in the history of the game of basketball has anyone devoted a single text to the art of rebounding. This work guides coaches to place a high degree of emphasis on this neglected phase of the game.

Graced With Opportunity by Kimati Ramsey

Graced With Opportunity is a six-month undated self-discovery journal. With a simple structured weekly format based on positive psychology research, the journal inspires readers to spend a few minutes each morning and evening disconnecting from their devices and reconnecting with their spirit through gratitude, self-awareness and productivity exercises.

ENGAGING WITH DAILY COACH

Join the Daily Coach community of leaders and learners.

Subscribe to our daily newsletter and explore more of our leadership lessons, tools, and resources for coaches, executives, and leaders at all levels at www.thedaily.coach.

www.ingramcontent.com/pod-product-compliance
Lightning Source LLC
Chambersburg PA
CBHW061940130526
44582CB00040B/29